GARDEN BAY STORIES

ET · IN · ARCADIA · EGO

Garden Bay Stories

The Shadow Head
and Other Tales of the Garden Bay

Richard Behrens

NINE MUSES BOOKS

Nine Muses Books

New England, USA

LizzieBordenGirlDetective.com
NineMusesBooks.com

© 2018 Nine Muses Books
© 2018 Anna Brindisi Behrens

ISBN-13: 978-0-9912784-1-1

Illustrations: Marc Reed, MarcReed.com
Book design: Stefani Koorey, peartree-press.com

For Richard (1964-2017)

His life was gentle, and the elements
So mixed in him that Nature might stand up
And say to all the world, "This was a man."

William Shakespeare

Also by Richard Behrens

Short Story Collections
Lizzie Borden: Girl Detective (2010, Pear Tree Press)
*The Audible Amnesiac and Other Lizzie Borden, Girl Detective
Stories* (2018, Nine Muses Books)
Garden Bay Stories (2018, Nine Muses Books)

Novels
The Minuscule Monk (2015, Nine Muses Books)

Non-Fiction Essay Collections
Moons and Monoliths (2018, Nine Muses Books)

Short Stories
(e-books by Nine Muses Books)
The Agitated Elocutionist
The Forlorn Maggie
The Purloined Curio
The Melancholy Scion
The Sculling Boat

Acknowledgements

Sincere gratitude to all those who contributed to Richard Behrens' GoFundMe page to make the posthumous publishing of his writing possible and fulfilling his wish to publish his stories of The Garden Bay. A heartfelt thank you to Susan Behrens, who masterfully edited Richard's unfinished works, and who provided personal knowledge of the Garden Bay Manor. We also gratefully acknowledge Catherine Behrens for her expert copy editing, and long-time friends Marc Reed for his beautiful cover design, and Stefani Koorey for her skillful book design.

TABLE OF CONTENTS

FOREWORD

The Garden Bay Manor was home to the Behrens family from 1962-1976. Richard, my brother, came along in 1964, and we moved from a one bedroom to a two bedroom apartment (still not enough space!).

Television sets were in almost every room, but so were books and LPs. Richard's playpen was set up near our living room's "wall of books" (we always had a wall of books); too close, in fact, for he would pluck books from the nearest shelf and tear up the pages. No one ever thought of just moving the playpen a foot or so to the left or right.

Memories of GBM and books and Richard: At age 9, Richard is sitting on the couch reading the Watergate transcripts to our grandmother, our regular baby sitter; we all are unpacking new purchases from our trips with our father to Manhattan's 4th Ave. (book row); Rich is flipping through coffee-table size books of the black and white horror films of the 1930s (lots of Frankenstein, and not the Fred Gwynne type).

Books were a large part of Richard's growing up. So was the Manor. That word never sounded grand to me, and it sure wasn't. The paint peeled off our bedroom walls, the boilers broke down with regularity, cars circled endlessly for a parking spot. When the Riker's Island Bridge went up, we had busloads of prisoners riding down our streets headed to the jail, and prisoners' visitors on the bus that took us to shopping and, later, high school. We were close enough to the Marine Air Terminal that we could easily spot the white bunny on Hugh Hefner's private black jet that time he landed there. We also easily habituated to the constant noise and soot of all those planes.

In the 1970s, girls caught Little League fever, and we spent time on the landfill called Elmjack. Boys discovered biceps and cars. Parking became even worse. But we could still ride our bikes (banana seats!) up to Ditmars. In the summer, the library was cool. In the winter, we stayed inside and listened to Beatles records. I listened to *Rubber Soul* for the first time in the Riker House (aka, the Smith House, Laurel being a friend). Now you need to make an appointment to take a tour, and then you only get access to the first floor.

GBM, with its underground trash cans, deep cellar pits, mock Tudor décor and brick door frames, perfect for standing in, pretending they were the sleep pods from *Lost in Space*. And we weren't doomed. We were close enough to "the city" but not bombarded with the crush of Manhattan. True, we had to walk to the bus that went to the train that went to the city. We were a two-fare zone. But we gladly made the trip often.

The area included some private houses, with porches and upstairs. Most of us squeezed into space too small for us, but we had trees outside the windows, the Good Humor guy on his bike, the mail delivered by 9am, crossing guards that knew our names, and the familiar faces of families that just never really thought about relocating.

Richard's wife Anna Brindisi Behrens has gone to great efforts to make Richard's GBM stories available to readers. These stories, vignettes, and poetry influenced by the GBM years demonstrate Richard's talents as a writer and observer. He starts with personal experiences as a young participant in a small-town culture in the middle of New York's most populated borough. These specific memories are woven into larger tales recognized by anyone from any American "manor" in the latter part of the 20th century, recognized and yet revealed for the first time. Richard makes us look back and reinterpret what we thought we knew. Go back to your old Polaroid snapshots, your vinyl 45s, that high school year book. Richard takes each item from his childhood and adolescence and, in a sense, rips up the pages so he can rewrite the tale to speak to each one of us.

Susan Behrens
Brooklyn, 2018

"Peace, be still!
The demons are no more aflight.
Darkest night is a warm mother's embrace.
Sleep, for only in your restful dreams
    can you see the garden I planted
       in those barren yards of youth."

Author Unknown

Garden Bay Short Stories

The Shadow Head

The Manor. 1973.

Dead voices whisper in the wind that comes in off the Bay, whipping across those sad fields behind the Little League diamonds and the tall weeds outlining the shore in the shadow of the prison island bridge. Spinning through those furrows and rocks, they bring their low cries of desolation down into the sewer culvert like haunted fingers reaching underneath the street where it happened and the line of row houses where I lived.

I remember the darkening streets of the Manor at twilight like a movie set that had been abandoned by the cast and crew, leaving behind the two-story attached houses with the mock Tudor trimming and the scattered apartment houses with their awnings and first story garages. At night it all lay inert under the stars, vast and alone.

That evening Mrs. Sackett was on the concrete porch in her rocking chair, facing the Bay. Every prison guard on the Island with a good pair of binoculars could, on a clear-air sundown, see her sitting with a little transistor radio and her big white orthopedic shoes. She listened to ball games, newscasts, interview shows. Never music. She didn't like any music except the remote songs in memory of her Scottish grandmother walking the Highlands, and that was on no station. So she sat with either the Mets or silence.

My grandmother lived upstairs and used to sit with Mrs. Sackett and talk about life during the war and old movies they had seen together. They talked about a time when everyone listened to the radio at night and cars looked the way they did in The Maltese Falcon. On a wall somewhere there is a photograph of the young pair of girls at Coney Island taken before my mother was born and they are smiling under chestnut hair. The night of the Shadow, my grandmother wasn't sitting next to Mrs. Sackett because she was in the hospital. I was told there was something wrong with her shoulder and she needed an operation, but I had heard her coughing from the bathroom and smelled the bitter medicine down her long corridor in the days before her leaving and knew that she had asked that I, Little Robbie, not be told that she may not return.

The Shadow came in off the public bus that brought visitors back from the Island at about eight o'clock, and right after the last commuters from the City had walked home from the express bus station and turned on the television lights in their living room windows, and the sun was slanting down across the rooftops ready to disappear. He must have gotten off right in front of the Parra house on Hazen Street, near the entrance to the bridge, tipping his cloth cap to the driver who didn't know he was an escaped prisoner. He must have walked along the crowded street that used to be an old post-road right by the old Riker place, a Dutch farmstead that was now in disrepair, and then along the cyclone fencing of the Little League fields, directly across from the row home where Mrs. Sackett sat, the only person to see him that night before his murder.

She said he had a dark cloud about him as thick as ink. No one knows where in the prison he got the clothes and the cap, or how he got onto the visitor bus, or even how he got past the checkpoints; but it remained that at seven-thirty by the clock he had been a convicted murderer in the exercise yard and then a half-hour later he was on the shore walking around in civilian clothes past Mrs. Sackett.

Perhaps she noticed him because people usually said hello to her and he was walking as if nothing about him was even there, as if his shadowy world didn't include anything that reflected light. Almost everyone stopped to talk to Mrs. Sackett, her being so tragic and all, with her feet swollen so many times their normal size that she could hardly move. After three husbands had died on her and her body had lost its shape and its health, all she was now resigned to doing was sitting on that porch facing the baseball fields and the Bay, a crone sentinel with a shock of white hair, a strange fragment of the old neighborhood (she had lived on this block even before the Manor had been built, when different homes faced the Bay at different angles to a different colored sky), holding off the darkness with a transistor radio. Then on this quiet evening that wasn't meant to be any different, the Shadow passed.

She thought, "This fella's goin' home or somethin'? I never seen him around."

We found out later from the police that he had killed a man in a bar over in Ozone Park and then when the cops came he put a gun to a woman's head before he was tackled by the bartender. This happened because the Shadow was either strung out on some drug that he needed to stop some illness or he was off some drug that he needed to stay sane, or something like that – either way it was an excuse that didn't go over in court and he had been sent out to the Island expecting to be put away in some maximum security prison somewhere for life.

Mrs. Sackett, who was the only witness to get a look at him, said that he was over six feet and big in limb. His face was smooth, his eyes kind of tender — you wouldn't know he had it in him. He had some sort of personal story that, supposedly, when you heard it you would start understanding him and feeling sorry for him and thinking: it's bad what he did, but I'd do the same thing if I suffered like he did. But no one I knew ever sat down to hear that story, being that he was a murderer and all. We just wanted to hate him because there was something missing in him. You have to have something missing in you to take another man's life and put a gun to a woman's head when it's not self-defense or fighting in a war.

After he passed by Mrs. Sackett, he wasn't seen by anyone else, and that was strange because it was after eight o'clock on a

Thursday night and there should have been at least a few people from the bars on 20th Avenue now stumbling home to face their families, but the streets played host to only one lone moving figure. Lights were flickering away in the house windows, the blue-and-white lights that shifted every time a new commercial came on. The Shadow had even passed by my living-room window where I was watching a movie, but I didn't know anything about it. Our house was on a curve as Mrs. Sackett's street bent away from the Bay. The Shadow just followed the sidewalk squares and passed out of Mrs. Sackett's sight. Now he was on my block.

My father was away that night and I was alone, so I easily could have been the Shadow's victim and only God knows why I wasn't. But I wasn't. It was like he knew where he wanted to go. Like he knew who was going to be at one particular apartment just two doors away from mine. The Sapios couple were out for the night and had hired a young high school girl, Sally Lear with the creamy face and the cutoff jeans, to watch their little boy Charlie.

She lived across the street and wanted to be a food scientist and listened to the Beatles on a stereo so loud it made my father close the window on a hot day. Little Charlie was in kindergarten and I didn't know very much about him or his family because he didn't have an older brother for me to run with. All I knew was that in their living room was a large picture of a full-sailed war ship like from an old English pirate movie over their couch. That was all I could see through their window while strolling outside.

My father was on a date in the city because he was single, so he wasn't there when I heard that something was happening up the block. The police sirens came in through the window screen and then I heard the neighbors talking in the street. I stuck my head out the screen and saw Mrs. Michaels watching the police cars.

She wasn't my mom. My mom was three thousand miles away in Los Angeles where she had gone after she left my father. Mrs. Michaels had been her best friend, and was the little piece of my mother that I still had, so when I saw her out there, I felt something like comfort. I couldn't remember being alive and not knowing Mrs. Michaels. My earliest memory is being underneath her kitchen table playing with her son. There was a comic book that we had cut with a pair of scissors and my father had called it Snip-snip. It was bad to go Snip-snip and the odor of Mrs. Michaels' coffee drifting down to the floor was always together with the memory of that comic book in pieces. Her legs and my mother's legs were on opposite sides of the table and the room smelled of coffee and cigarettes.

"Your dad home?" Mrs. Michaels said, surprised, and then realized I was all alone and said, "My God," and had me buzz her into the front hallway. She put on my coat and took me outside and I could see the police lights flashing colors against the apartment fronts and hear the hiss of the radio static and more sirens in the distance.

Everyone was out there, in their bathrobes, in their slippers, in their after-work shirts and blue jeans. Some older kids on bicycles were keeping their distance but peered toward the semi-circle of cops and the two squad cars outside the Sapios apartment. We saw something on the ground and when Mrs. Michaels realized what it was, she brought me back inside and sat and waited with me for my father to come home.

"It's a bad man," she said. "He tried to hurt Sally but she's all right."

"What bad man?"

"From the Island."

That was all she had to say and I didn't want to hear any more. The Island was that shark pen across the Bay where the bad men were kept inside by guns and if they ever broke out it was my neighborhood they would hit first. We were taught in school to watch out for men coming out of that water. Sometimes they drifted over in rubber rafts smuggled in by crooked guards. Sometimes we found the rafts deflated by the waterfront like used condoms. We only knew condoms from the used ones we found down by the mud flats, didn't even know what they were. If you mentioned the word "condom" to us, we would explain they were little rubber things that people leave by mudflats. So we thought the rubber raft looked like a big condom. We always feared the bad men coming out of the water, dripping oil from their hair, stinking in rat stuff from the sewer, and coming down our block.

We learned the word "correction" and I always wondered why the people on the Island were "correct" if they were so bad. My friends and I would stand where the street curved around a patch of lawn facing the baseball field and watch the prison bus drive to the Bridge at the end of the post road. We'd see the silhouettes in the rear of the bus; some of them were guards holding rifles up past their shoulders, all behind the heavy screens. And us, knock-kneed little white kids with fathers who drove trucks and taxi cabs and worked the cash registers at the supermarket, us standing there in our summer shorts, pointing fingers at the passing vehicles and crying, "Ah-ha! You got caught!" and the smallest of us saying, "Ga cha!" and trying to make the men on the bus feel terrible about themselves. But a heavy man with big nostrils thrust his face against the grating and said in a rasp, "You fucking kids! I'm going to kill you when I get out!" And we went silent very fast.

So whenever there was talk of a Shadow coming out of the water or creeping across the Bridge, we thought it was the "I'm-Going-To-Kill-You-When-I-Get-Out-Man" arriving to make good on his promise. His face came rising over the edge of our blankets at night, not a face really but a black mass, the shape of a face, or a head, no expression, no emotion, like a past rage had wiped out all his features. Perhaps just eyes peering, red-veined, pained eyes that wanted only to kill anything alive that it didn't respect.

That's how, after seeing the Shadow lying in the gutter surrounded by police and neighbors, after realizing that the man was dead outside the Sapios apartment, I knew the Shadow could only have been after little Charlie Sapios, not Sally Lear, because Charlie was one of those kids who stood on the corner on the open lawn and said, "You got caught" as the corrections bus drove past.

Little Charlie told the story to his friends the next day: "And the bad man came and then the Twins came and they went Dooosh! Dooosh!" hurtling fists in the air, "and then the bad man was on the ground. And I saw blood." That was the story he told and exactly how he told it. He wasn't even frightened that he had seen two grown men kill another man violently, because the Twins had protected him when he was in danger and besides he had seen it all before on television. Little Charlie was known for watching cop shows and was excited that the flashing lights and the uniformed men were giving him so much attention. One man had a flip pad and a pencil just like on television and told Little Charlie that he was a brave boy, braver than anyone he had known who had gone to Vietnam. Charlie wasn't scared; he was laughing like he had just seen a good movie on the television set.

The Twins were the Pantios boys from upstairs where Sally was baby-sitting for Little Charlie. They didn't have the same face but they had shared the same womb and were never seen apart from each other, except when they went out with girls. They were talking to the police as well, one of them sitting on a milk box on the porch and drinking from a blue paper cup like someone had run to the candy store to get him some coffee, and the other hopping on his feet with a blanket over his shoulders like he was trying to keep warm. Between the coffee and the hopping I started to believe that killing a man made you cold and you had to get yourself warm somehow. The cop talking to them was pointing at the gutter and the body, which was now under a blanket, and laughing a bit. I'll never forget how the cop smiled and laughed while pointing at the body, especially since he was standing in front of the men who had done the killing.

The Twins told their story too, but it took longer to tell. They heard the banging, the Shadow pounding on the windows and the front door, snarling, "Let me in!" and Sally screaming, too paralyzed to even touch the telephone, although she had time to do so. Perhaps she thought that the cops would take forever to get there and by that time the Shadow would be in the living room so why spend what might be her last few moments dialing the telephone and talking to an operator while she could put those moments to screaming so loudly the neighbors would hear and arrive, hopefully, almost immediately — unlike the cops.

And indeed the Twins heard the screams and came down the stairs into the front hallway where they saw a thin, pale-faced man in a cloth cap and dungarees attacking the door to the downstairs apartment like it was the embodiment of everything he despised and was disgusted with, all the rage and pain of the bars and steel plates and locked doors that kept him from the outside world, the world for which no man could fault him for desiring, all there behind that barrier put there by the police, by judges, by the disgust of society. All his rage and pain were embodied in that door.

And within: the little boy and the young high school girl who were innocent. The Shadow knew that, but he saw their innocence as something bitterly wrong, something that needed to be changed. What could he have done if he had gotten past that door? Little Charlie didn't know, but perhaps Sally Lear did. I didn't see her in the crowd but as Mrs. Michaels and I got closer to their front porch I caught a glimpse of her through the window, standing between her anxious parents and circled by detectives, framed by that large painting of the ship over the couch. She was crying and blowing into a tissue and hanging down her head and when they weren't talking to her, she looked up at that painting like she was staring past it and trying to see something that wasn't in the room. The painting was probably a cheap gift from a savings bank when the Sapios couple had opened an account. The ship rose upwards in a bloom of cannons and masts like a full-feathered bird strutting its colors.

The Twins didn't think anything about what the Shadow had felt before they killed him. They just called out, "Hey," and he bolted right past them into the street. The Twins followed and one of them, who knows which one, picked up Little Charlie's skate that was lying on the lawn and hurled it in the dim twilight and miraculously struck the Shadow just above one of his ears, causing him to pause, then stumble and hit the dirt beneath the grass. They say he yelled out, "Not now!" which the Twins said was a cowardly way of getting out of a fight, but I think he meant that something had started in his head that was bad and strange and the Shadow knew that he didn't stand a chance of getting away with the roller-coaster started inside his head by the impact of the skate against his skull.

Then they were on him, beating him with something, I never heard what. Some say it was a crowbar, others say it was a plank of wood. I think it was Little Charlie's skate, because what else could they have found on the front lawn? Whatever it was, and it certainly wasn't their fists, it made his skull crack and the sidewalk bloody. They beat him even after he was dead, they say. But I never saw it. I just heard the yells and the police sirens after it was all over and then Mrs. Michaels came by and realized my father wasn't home and waited with me.

He came in through the door confused, thinking there had been a robbery and when we told him what happened, he got all dark, thinking it could have been his own son and why in God's name did he leave him alone like that. But when you are raising a child on your own, you can't be watching him every minute, and if you can't get a baby-sitter, you'd better be careful where you leave him and at what time of the day. The world wasn't safe and the Manor even less so, ever since they put in that extra bar which brought in the men from the other side of the airport.

So he sat me down and tenderly tried to communicate his guilt and regret: "I was trying to find you another mother," he said, and then I realized that he smelled of cologne and his hair was brushed neatly and he had on one of those starched shirts that he only wore to PTA meetings. He hadn't been on a date since my mother left and this was a big night for him. He leaves his son alone so he could take a woman to a restaurant and think about himself for one evening, and while he's gone a Shadow escapes from the Island and tries to kill a girl and a boy across the street, passing so close the killer walks right by his son's window to get there. Something was holding him back, he must have felt. Something didn't want him to live a different life.

A knock on the door: it was Mrs. Sackett. She had hobbled around the corner with her walker, a long way for someone with legs like hers, and wanted to know if I was all right, little Robbie who was so helpless because he didn't know what he was doing half the time. I told her, "Yes," and then stood behind my father because Mrs. Sackett scared me. I thought she had these eyes that looked down a wind tunnel into a place where no one else could see. She smelled of old furniture and dusty end tables polished with lemon-oil and a stained cleaning rag.

My father sat her down in the living room and made some tea for everyone and we all sat around trying not to pay much mind to the red lights of the cop cars outside, or the muttering of the neighbors gathering around the death site. My father and Mrs. Sackett and Mrs. Micheals drank their tea like it was a natural evening and that my mother was still sitting between them.

"I saw him," Mrs. Sackett said. "I saw him walk in off the bus mindin' his own business, and he went right by me and didn't even say hello. He had a hat on but when I was outside I didn't see no hat. I wonder where that hat is? I wonder if you'll find it in the bushes tomorrow. "

"Maybe," my father said, staring into space.

"I wonder where he got that hat in the first place. He came in off the Island. He got into some clothes and stepped right onto the bus and came off like it was nothing."

The deflated rafts in the shifting reeds where the sewer entered the Bay. The stick hitting the ball on the diamond sending a sound that cracked open and echoed in the culvert. The pilots in their planes tearing the sky.

"Is that right?" Mrs. Michaels said. "What we doing raising our boys near a terrible place like this?"

"When I get remarried," my father said, "I'm going to take Robbie away from here. We're going to go live in Forest Hills."

Mrs. Michaels huffed. "And what kind of woman you going to marry could afford to live in Forest Hills?"

"Combined income," he said, shrugging his shoulders.

When they finished their tea, they walked out into the street helping Mrs. Sackett. The crowds had moved away, but there were a few people still left looking at something on the ground.

"He don't want to see this," Mrs. Sackett said.

"I do," I said. So my father took me across the street, leaving the ladies behind.

It wasn't a person, it was a chalk outline. The arms and legs were at all crazy angles and near the head was a big dark splotch that still glistened under the street lamps. It looked like a cartoon of a man with a crazy balloon hat on his head running for a bus.

My father stood behind me and put his hands on my shoulders. I didn't look up but I reached up and touched his hand. It felt warm. It was my father's hand.

The night was getting darker, if such a thing was possible.

The outline stayed there for a few weeks before someone ripped up the tape and the rest of it faded. The kids made up some games around it, sort of like hopscotch, but with no formal rules other than you had to jump from arm to leg and then land on the head with your right foot. We found variations on these rules, but it always had to do with that muddy smeared head being "Safe." If you had your feet planted firmly on it, no one could harm you.

Big Brian tormented little kids by making them lick the head. No one tasted anything but hard dirty concrete, but the thought of tasting the sidewalk where blood and brains once were made them cry and run home, with Brian laughing so hard he would immediately look around for his next victim and we would scatter like buzzing flies.

I didn't find any of it scary, since the outline was fading from day to day and would soon be gone, especially with the August rain. What did frighten me were the Twins. They never really talked to me, but I kept my distance. I stood across the street and stared at them playing handball against the side of a house, never being able to put out of my mind that I was looking at two men who had killed another man, and not just killed him, but mutilated him. When they could have just grabbed him and waited for the police to come, they forced him to the ground and beat him with a blunt instrument until his head was all mush. No one but me seemed to mind. Maybe the thought of what the Shadow could have done to Little Mike and Sally Lear was so terrible, and what with his previous murder in the Ozone Park bar and the poor thought of that woman with the gun pressed to her head, maybe all that was enough to purge the Pantios Twins of their violent sin. Folks felt safer knowing that living with them were two wild young boys who were capable of throwing a man to the ground and beating him until he no longer had a head. They even got more women into bed because they were heroes. I was the only one in the Manor who was afraid of them.

Behind the Riker house was an old graveyard where George Washington's personal doctor, or something, was buried. The small yard of fading headstones was wedged between the old house and the trucking yard, dense with overhang from the willow and the oak. The people who lived there would yell at you if you set foot on their property, although none of us really wanted to. We were told by someone, I think it was Big Brian, that the Shadow was in there, lurking about, knocking on the doors of the graves like he had knocked on Sally Lear's door, asking to be let in. He was all tormented because he didn't want to go back across the Bridge to the Island, and he couldn't go forward into the grave. Besides, all those ghosts were colonial soldiers who had fought bravely for their families against injustice. They didn't want some dark, dirty murderer who wanted to rape girls living with them. The poor Shadow was now trapped between two worlds and was said to spend the night in the sewer culvert with the rats and the floating condoms. During the day, he wandered the rows of stones, screaming, begging to be let in.

Of course, I was also afraid of the spot where the murder had taken place because it was a cluster of insane energy. I also knew he didn't live in the sewer culvert at all, but since he couldn't get into a proper grave at night, he would go back to the asphalt where he died and lay down, a soul that never made it to any afterlife, still raging, still angry, still trying to get through the door that would lead him to freedom.

Then one day I was sitting with Little Charlie on an oil drum outside the fence to the ball field, staring up the block, perhaps waiting for another Corrections bus to speed by around the curve on its way to the Island so we could stare at the silhouettes in the back of the bus and wonder which one would escape next and come after us.

Then Charlie's eyes widened and he sighed. "Well, he's gone," he said.

"Who?" I said.

He pointed up the block to where the Shadow had been beaten to death.

"What?" I said.

"He just got up and walked away," Charlie said.

I thought of what Little Charlie had said, and what he claims he saw as he looked up the street; the chalk outline got right up, blasted head and all, and walked off, angry at being a spectacle, stomped on by kids, played with and teased, mocked and gawked at, rumored about, and so it decided to walk off just as smoothly as it walked off the bus that night and came banging at the Sapios house to get past that locked door. And I looked down the block and heard the death echo of the wind through the sewer under our feet, spilling back into the Bay, answering the blast of the yard siren off on the Island, echoing, thundering across the water, calling the lonely spirit home.

And I believed him.

Buried Voices

1974. Billy Delaware lived in the Manor away from the row homes in a four-story, multi-family apartment building with a plastic awning over the front door, a rectangle of a house that rose above the tree tops and the phone lines. He had been a communications specialist in Vietnam, so in those days he was tinkering with radios and tape recorders in the first floor garage below his apartment on a large table that had once housed his father's toy train set. It was a hippy garage with a peace sign on the wall and an American flag and all sorts of tools tossed about and paperback books tumbling out of cardboard boxes. Billy was a peaceful guy even though he had been in the war and to this day anything with a chestnut pony tail and a goatee and an army jacket reminds me of a man who had done bad things but later thought about it and decided never to do them again.

There were some antiques on that table: reel-to-reel tape recorders, big suitcase-sized ones that were as heavy as the old radios that he dissected. Some looked like dark wooden boxes when closed. Others were sleeker with shiny silver finish and nicely contoured dials. We called them the sound machines because they captured the sounds that were made around the microphone. You could talk into the metal bulbs and your voice would go along the wire into the box and then later you could play the tape back and hear yourself as if someone else was talking.

I had only heard my voice on tape once before. On a lost 1971 age-seven afternoon I stood before a record-making machine in an arcade on the Coney Island Boardwalk and spoke into a plastic horn. Then I went home with a small vinyl record that I played on my father's stereo and heard a strange crackling high-pitched whine that could have been my voice accompanied by the bells and whistles of the arcade around me. The novelty of it all made me play it back several dozen times, marveling that it was me on the other side of the speaker, and then the record wore out. The needle had flattened the groove, and the cheap piece of trash I had paid a dime for was now unplayable.

But Billy's sound machines were different. You could talk for the whole length of the tape as it unspooled off the reel, and then when it finished and flapped against the play head, you could turn the reel around and talk all you wanted to for the length of the second side. You could talk for hours into these machines, and then listen to yourself for hours.

I had written my first short story, typing it out on my father's manual typewriter, the one with the weak W, and called it The Revenge of the Mummy. Billy laughed and slapped my back. "What's he want revenge for?"

"They put him in a coffin when he wasn't dead. And they cut off his tongue. He can't speak anymore."

"Then why do you have him yelling at the museum guards?" he asked. Then added, "In Egyptian."

I was baffled on that one and I had to rethink the story. That made Billy Delaware my first editor, and not a shabby one. I turned on the big wooden tape recorder and spontaneously self-edited as I read from the typing paper, cutting out all the speaking parts that I had created for Im-Ho-Tet VI the Mad Mummy ("Don't come if you're chicken," the movie poster would read). The story took up one third of the tape side and for the rest of the tape you could hear Billy making me say funny things, asking me how old I was and all sorts of inappropriate requests like asking me to fart for the microphone.

"We don't have a recorded history of farting," he mused. "We have presidential speeches and baseball games preserved forever on tape, but we don't have any documented history of the good honest farting of the common man."

"It's too personal," I argued.

"Ah, but the human voice, that's the one that's personal. You speak with the same voice you confess love to a woman, with the same mouth that kisses your mother before going to bed, with the same tongue that tastes all the food that you put into your body. When you speak, people look at your mouth, and see that moving fleshy organ that will do the most intimate acts you can imagine throughout your lifetime, and you use it publicly like no one would ever wonder what else you've done with it."

I looked down at the tape reel that carried my voice as if it were a picture of me coming out of the shower. "Can you get rid of it?" I asked. I didn't know the word for "delete" yet.

He chuckled. "Don't worry about what you said on there. We were just horsing around. But be careful. Remember, the Indians were afraid the camera would steal something from inside of them; well, the sound machine can steal from you as well. Someone else can have your voice and it would no longer belong to you. The words have been stolen from your mouth. He could chop up the tape and make you say things you never said. Wouldn't that be a violation?"

I was ten years old and didn't really know what he was saying, but it was recorded on that thin brown strip of tape and years later I listened to it repeatedly and memorized the whole speech, fleshy organ and all. Billy had a big mind that thought about things like that. He also listened to opera which was always coming from the house upstairs. Every time I think of Billy Delaware I think of those Italian voices coming across the radio. They drifted down into the garage and sometimes got onto the tape I was making. You listen today and you can hear Verdi voices in the distance like lonesome train whistles beyond the fields singing in Italian.

Those tapes lay for decades on a shelf in an unheated garage and turned brittle and fell apart. My voice, and my stupid mummy story, lay dormant for decades. All I had to do was take them down and put them in a warm closet to protect them, but I didn't, and they died, and my first short story with it: "The Revenge of the Mummy."

All the trouble started because Mike and Jamie and Kevin and some of the others from the Manor houses used to come over to Billy Delaware's garage to play with the tape recorders. I had gotten the idea from Billy to cut up the tapes and we'd do little skits and cut in sounds from pop records. Like we'd have someone saying, "What do you need?" and then we'd cut in John Lennon singing "HELP! I need somebody!" We'd play it back and think it was all very funny. Crazy mixed-up tapes we called them.

Big Ben lived around the corner from the Delawares and he'd come out to get into his blue fin-tailed sedan and he'd look at us and maybe wave or click his finger off his forehead like he was saluting with one finger. He was big and when he'd get into the car we'd all stop and look and wait to see the driver's side of the car bounce down onto the ground and then up into the air as he adjusted himself in the seat. There was something dirty about him, and his car felt that way too. It was about twenty years old, and already one scout from the film studios up Steinway Street had offered to rent it from him for a film that took place in 1955. Big Ben didn't want nobody touching his car and he turned down the offer. He was unemployed most of the time but we didn't know what he did with himself when he drove off in his car.

One time he ran out of money and couldn't put gas into the car. He lived with his ex-wife's mother who was in her eighties and he was worried that the old woman would have a heart attack and have to get to a hospital at a time when there was no gas in the car. My father told him he could call the emergency number and they would come get her, but Big Ben felt like that was begging someone to help and he had too much pride for that. Then he got a job as a security guard at the aviation plant on Northern Boulevard and there was some money coming in and he put some gas in the car. Some mornings we'd see him leave his apartment in his uniform, a blue shirt and striped pants, and he would tell us he had a gun at work but he wasn't allowed to take it home. If he could, he would show it to us.

Then, we wanted Big Ben to do some voices for us on the crazy mixed-up tapes. He did it to make us laugh, but he didn't seem too happy. On the tape you could hear him walking away from the microphone saying, "You got that, you retards?" At the time we didn't think twice about someone saying something like that, but now I feel that it's a terrible thing to say to a bunch of children. Big Ben had a son of his own and should have known better. The last time we heard about Big Ben's son was just before I moved away. The kid had been arrested for drug dealing and was on the prison island. We heard he became the ping-pong champ of his ward.

It had been a mistake bringing Big Ben over to be in the crazy mixed-up tapes. It got him thinking about Billy Delaware, and once we saw the two of them talking in front of the house, and Billy didn't look very happy. Big Ben was saying something harsh and hitting his fist against the front railing. They'd get into some sort of argument and you can tell both of them were trying hard to keep their voices down so we couldn't hear them. Then Big Ben wagged his finger in Billy's face and then turned to us and made a strange gesture like he was firing a bullet from his finger, then walked away without saying goodbye to anyone. He hobbled back to his house and slammed the door. Billy stood for a full minute just looking at the ground, then looked up at us and gave a small smile, then went into his garage and disappeared up into the house. We didn't know what they had been talking about, but it certainly looked like Big Ben had shouted the last word.

That afternoon, Mike and I hung out on the yard facing the baseball fields trying to figure out what Big Ben had talked about that made Billy so rattled. If only there had been a tape recorder between them and they were talking into the microphone, we could play back the tapes and listen and learn all the secrets that they were hiding from us. There had to be some way to place those tape recorders in people's homes so we could learn all their secrets, and then cut all the voices up onto a giant crazy mixed-up tape that would tell the story of the Manor in sound, a vast collage of shameful secrets, unspoken surprises, and dangerous stories. What did people say to each other when the last bus from the train stop had scattered the street sounds to silence and the television lights were flickering in the living-room windows and the sun had slanted behind the old Riker house putting our dreams to rest for another night on earth?

That summer there was a strange black car that used to come round and park in front of the little league field by the bay inlet. Big Ben would go to it and a passenger window would roll down and then Big Ben would talk to someone for a while, then give a friendly wave of goodbye and walk back to his house. One evening, when Mike and I were coming back around the corner across from where the gate was to the bay inlet, we saw the car, and Big Ben was standing there. Then the back door opened and two men in suits got out, shaking hands with him, and then they stood and talked for a while. Mike and I stood in the shadow of a Manor house, making sure that we weren't seen, and we could tell that Big Ben and the two guys in suits were looking around to make sure that no one could see them either.

They talked by the fence for a while, and Mike and I were scared. Then Big Ben took out some sort of tool and he walked up to the fence and with the tool he cut the chain on the fence. Then he opened the fence, and the black car drove into the dark interior of the field near the bay inlet. Big Ben closed the fence behind it and was about to walk away when he saw us. We had tried to run down the street but he saw us and he crossed the street. We were standing frozen when he walked up to us.

"You fucking kids didn't see nothing!" he said, and whacked Mike across the cheek like he was his father who had a right to do something that harsh. Mike cried a little, but Big Ben stared him down, which made him stop. "What did you see?" he asked.

"Nothing," Mike said.

Then Big Ben threatened to hit him again and we started running. We ran back to my apartment and stood in the front hallway for a while crying and telling each other that we didn't see anything and that nothing bad would happen to us. But then we started wondering exactly what we had seen.

"That's the place where the escaped prison guys come over," Mike said.

Across the bay, the yard siren cried out at noon and in the clouds at night we could see the search beams scanning the walls. My father called it a "correctional facility" but we knew it as the place where the bad men were held back with guns and walls and barbed wire. If it weren't for those defenses, they would come across the bay in a flotilla of rubber rafts, creep from the oily water, and kill us in our sleep. The summer before, a bad man from the Island had even gotten his hands on some civilian clothes and walked right out the front door, onto the shuttle bus, and had tried to kill the family across the street. He was beaten to death by the neighbors and his chalk outline still lay in the street where we played some bizarre form of hop-scotch, treating the dark and muddy stain around the head as the final landing spot of our hopping. Our small lives were shadowed by an endless vigil against the bad men from the Island. The thought that Big Ben knew something about this or was planning to help one of them escape made him just as bad as them.

The next morning we were back in Billy's garage playing around with the tapes, doing fake interviews like we were Walter Cronkite, pretending that one of us had seen John F. Kennedy shot from a grassy knoll. It was Kevin who said, "Oh shit," and pointed to the street. Big Ben was coming over, walking right in front of the traffic as if defying it to hit him; then he came right into the garage like he had stormed past some invisible line that should have stopped him. We thought he was after us at first, but he looked down with his craggy face and asked, "Where's Delaware?"

Billy came down and tried to reason with Big Ben, but the man began to berate him. Then Billy pointed to us and told Big Ben that we should leave, and he agreed. We bolted out of there, leaving behind the tape recorder that we had been playing with. It was still turning on the spindles and recording everything that was going on inside the garage, and while the big man shook down the small man, shouting and rampaging, threatening and punishing, the tape was spinning. We came back after five minutes and saw the garage empty. No Big Ben. He must have withdrawn back to his apartment and the secrecy of his most private space and his very private mother-in-law. We saw the tape still spinning and it was Mike who turned it off, dismounted both reels, tore the tape where it had stopped playing, and took one of the reels and slipped it into his pants. Then we threw the other reel, with only half the tape on it, back onto the workbench and ran as fast as we could.

We ran as far as the creek along the little league field and hid inside the overhang of the weeping willow. The blare of the yard siren off on the Island gave us a strange comfort as if all that violence was still contained off-shore. We lay on our backs and watched the commercial planes out of the airport cut lines through the afternoon sky.

God bless the pilots in their planes, we thought and then looked at each other sadly. We still couldn't understand the world and lived in fear of the grown-ups who had betrayed our trust in them. The pilots, we figured, were better men than that. Everyday people trusted them with their lives, and since the pilots were on the same airplane as their passengers, there was no way they were going to let that plane go down. The strange men from the car who had talked to Big Ben that night wouldn't think twice about jumping out in a parachute while all the passengers plunged to their deaths. That seemed to us to be the great dividing line between one half of humanity and the other. Maybe we weren't too far off the truth.

I had forgotten that Mike had the tape down his pants, I had forgotten that we had escaped, and that Big Ben was back in his house, but all I could think of was the black car in the dark evening, a wire cutter opening the gates, the rush of the wind in the weeds and the smell of rat shit coming off the bay inlet. The serenity of the willow, the listing of the tall grass, and the slanting of the sunlight through the oak branches, were all expired in my mind in the wake of the hulking shape that loomed in silhouette before me, the savage mountain of a man who would hurt me without thinking if it meant giving him some advantage in whatever petty and violent game he was playing.

I covered my eyes, hoping that he couldn't see me, afraid more for my friend who lay beside me in some mock funereal pose. There was danger in the wind, in the siren from the prison island, in the shadows that nested in the basements, the cellar pits, the garage workshops and the dusty dark apartment interiors of the Manor. A lucid fear lay in waiting and my small hands couldn't cover enough of my open eyes.

The summer ended and we had one more week before going to fifth grade, except for Jamie who was starting third. Our bicycle tires were flattened and our sneakers were too tight on our feet. Best of all, my birthday ended the summer and I had never known a school day coinciding with it. A trip to Adventurer's Inn or Coney Island or Far Rockaway always presented itself, often my grandmother taking me, on a rare occasion my parents, before my mother had departed.

Coney Island was a bus and a train ride away, and took almost an hour to get there. My grandmother had known it when it was vibrant and alive; now it was filthy and broken with motorcycle gangs and drug deals going down off the boardwalk but there were still a few creaky old rides and a sideshow with a gorilla act and a midget who lay down on a bed of nails. It was the only place I had known in Brooklyn and to my imagination it was a magical place where I spent my birthday that summer. I walked on the beach with my grandmother, who stared off into the distance toward Staten Island remembering something that she did not share with me.

On the bus ride home, the joyous thrill of the day lasted as a buzz inside my heart and when my grandmother left me in the living-room, I was elated in a way only such a time, age and place could bring when filtered through memory. But the sun had darkened and a wind was picking up, knocking the window frames and whistling through the cellar pits, that haunting moan that was the background radiation of my life. A rustle of cicadas burst through the air, then fell to silence as my father emerged from his bedroom, his face slack and perplexed. I started to tell him about the amusement park and the midget but he said to me soberly, "Come with me" and led me with a large hand back into the bedroom.

On the dresser he had set up a tape recorder, and had threaded a tape through it and the side of the reel was already half played.

Immediately, I recognized the machine from Billy Delaware's garage, and although he hadn't turned it on yet, I knew what he had heard on the tape. Not the exact words, but I knew that he had been listening to Billy's fight with Big Ben and that my father now knew more about what had been said that day than I had.

"Where did you get this?" he asked me. I didn't have an answer for him, but finally gathered enough presence of mind to ask, "Where did you get it?"

He looked back at me startled, then seemed to see sense in my question. "Mr. Cosmopolis gave it to me. He got it from Mike. Your voices are at the front of the tape." He thought inwardly for a moment as if debating the crossing of some delicate line, and then he said, "Were you there when this happened?"

I told him that we had run from the garage before they started talking and that seemed to relax him a bit. But then he ordered me to get my cap and told me that we were going for a walk. I immediately thought of Mike. Was my father taking me to the Cosmopolis house? Or even more dangerous: to Big Ben's? As we rounded the corner, I studied my father's face, trying to divine what frame of mind was driving him, what questions in him were so demanding he was willing to bring his own son to the monster that had put those words on that tape.

We found Big Ben in his front yard, his huge belly squeezed into a tank top, his spindly legs stomping on some cardboard he had just broken down from boxes. When he saw us coming, he stood like a frozen statue, staring forward with a still face; then he kicked his cardboard aside and walked to his fence gate as if preparing to defend his territory against some form of invasion. He had the solid stance of a wrestler and that impenetrable squat face with half-closed eyes as we came to a halt before him.

"I want to know what you did to my boy," my father asked boldly.

"I didn't do nothing to him," came the answer.

"Look, Ben, I know what you do around here and personally, I don't care about what you get involved in. Just don't involve my boy."

"I didn't," came the next reply. "Your boy's not involved in nothing."

My father stared back, silent for a moment as he tried to

interpret what he was hearing. There was a judgment to be made as to Big Ben's sincerity. Nothing could resolve this issue except some form of instinctual faith that my father had to decide upon or forever wallow in confusion and doubt. Finally, he said, "I don't want you near him."

"I don't want to be near him," Big Ben said starkly. "Get lost now, so I won't be near him."

My father's courage was wearing off, and he began to look frightened, so he took my hand, turned and began to go away when Big Ben said unexpectedly from behind, "Break your fucking neck next time."

We kept walking, quicker now, and my father's hand tightened on mine, so hard it was hurting. We walked as far as the candy store on 20th Avenue and my father bought me ice cream and a soda. We sat at the counter and before we left he bought me a comic book. We didn't speak to each other the entire time, not even after we got home.

Kevin was the first one to start talking about Big Ben burying a body in the landfill behind the little league. He got it into his head and once it was in there, it was difficult to dislodge. Perhaps he saw something on television, perhaps he heard it from someone else, but he passed it to us. It made sense to us at first because no one had seen Big Ben's mother in a long time; she never came out of the apartment and during the day when Ben was at work, there wasn't any sign of life in any of the windows facing the street.

We sat next to our bikes over near the bush that was cut like a flying saucer and talked an entire afternoon when we could have been riding. We would get into serious trouble if anyone knew what we knew. And if we kept it all to ourselves, it would somehow damage us. But we didn't know anything. The men in the car had never been round before and Big Ben looked like he respected them, like they outranked him in some invisible army. Perhaps Big Ben was doing something for them or else they would hurt him. Perhaps he was scared too.

That afternoon we saw Big Ben taking out his garbage and we stared at him from across the street. He knew we were there, but he ignored us. Mike could have sworn that before he went back in he gave us a quick wink with one eye, but I didn't see that. He disappeared back into his apartment and we dared each other to check what he had thrown out. Maybe there were clues in there.

After sundown, we stole the garbage can and brought it to Mike's basement and went through it with a flashlight. There were disgusting remains of meals, old newspapers, a broken light bulb, and some crushed pizza boxes, even a dirty old sock with a golf ball in it. At the very bottom we found a piece of paper that had some handwriting on it, but it looked like notes from a telephone call about a hospital. Hoping that we had proof that Big Ben's mother had gotten sick and had been removed somewhere, we kept the piece of paper and then put the garbage can back. For the rest of the evening, long after we had gone back to our separate homes and were watching television with our parents, we were all wondering if we had put the can back in the same position in which we had found it.

Thoughts of school and anticipation of what fifth grade would be like gave us some distraction from the fear of Big Ben. My grandmother took me clothes shopping and then got my back-to-school supplies, composition notebook, rubber book strap, several colored folders and three-ringed binder. I also got a larger satchel to keep it all in. At my grandmother's dinner table I put it all together and she took a picture of me and then I ran back to my house, nervous and excited, waiting to show my father how big I was getting and how I deserved to be promoted to fifth grade. But as I approached the apartment, I slowed down and stared at the police car that was double-parked right in front of our garbage cans.

Inside, my father was talking to two police officers, and none of them seemed too happy about my sudden appearance. My father told me to go to my room, he would be with me shortly, and then he finished up his muttered business which I heard through the door, but couldn't catch the words. The police went silently away and my father came into my room, sat on the edge of my bed and tried to smile.

"I just want you to know," he told me, "that I gave them the tape that I got from Mike's dad."

"You got it from Mike's dad? It belonged to Billy."

"I know," he said, raising his hands. "Billy is just as concerned as I am and he's spoken to the police as well. But it's all out of our hands now; the police will take care of everything. There's other stuff they found."

I didn't respond, I just stared at him. My lips were pressed together, the only sign that I was unhappy. Perhaps there were tears in my eyes, I don't remember. Inside, I was collapsing; something was collapsing. None of this was supposed to be happening. The tape recording was supposed to go away and vanish, be something of the past. The voices would still be on it, but if no one played them through a machine, nothing would be heard. Anything that Big Ben told Billy about what was happening wasn't for anyone to hear. It wasn't supposed to be recorded in the first place. It wasn't supposed to be heard by Mike's father, and my father, and now the New York City police. Soon hundreds of people would be hearing it, and Big Ben would find out how it reached their ears.

"He's going to kill us," I told my father quietly.

"No, he's not. They don't even have to use the tape to put that man away. Just don't tell anyone, not even your friends."

I asked a question that I didn't want to ask. "What did he do?"

"Don't worry about it. When you're older maybe I'll tell you." He looked up at the darkening window shade. "Maybe after we move out of here…"

"Do we have to move?" I asked.

He stroked my hair with a firm hand. "We should, soon. And not just because of Ben."

"What about Grandma?" I asked. "She'll be here…" "With him," was my unfinished thought.

He said thinly, "I don't know about her." Then he went away and I lay on the bed watching the dull sunlight against the ceiling, thinking of the cellar pits and basements of the Manor that were good places to hide. I thought of the pilots in their planes overhead, and how they were above it all but could know the secrets of all the small lives in the scattering of housing they saw far below their wings.

Morning session began on the third floor of the school, which meant every day at lunch I had to walk down two flights of stairs. Also, from the window of our classroom, I could see the tops of the houses on 80th Street. Beyond that was the bay, the airport runways, the prison island. We took a field trip to LaGuardia and came back with Pan American pilot wings clipped to our shirts. The New York Times got delivered to our classroom every morning and we had to do reports on the lead stories. I wrote about President Nixon and how he had ended the Vietnam War.

Reading about the war and the events in Saigon evoked another war, the one that was raging inside Big Ben's head. When I tried to imagine the people of Vietnam who were trapped between two armies, I saw them walking the streets in the shadow of several Big Bens. Reading about President Nixon and his use of tape recorders heightened my sense that reels of recording tape were bad, that bad things were on them, that people would go to great lengths to prevent anyone from hearing the voices that they contained. Nixon wouldn't hand the tapes over to the Supreme Court, but my father had handed over the Big Ben tape without hesitation. I didn't know how I felt about that.

After one week of school, and this was definitely a Friday afternoon, I came home and fell asleep in my father's bed. Friday was his late day because he did volunteer work and he wasn't expected until dinner time. When I woke up, I was disoriented, and didn't know where I was, or what time it was. Stumbling off the bed, I fell on the floor and saw a box that my father had put under there. I pulled it out and opened it, and found the reel of tape. The Big Ben tape. Somehow my father had gotten it back from the police and was holding onto it.

It burned in my hands. It was an obscene package, something that wasn't supposed to exist.

I pushed the box back under the bed and fled to my room with the tape. I hid it under a load of clothing in the closest, and then crawled into bed. When my father got home, I pretended to be tired and then lay all afternoon and evening listening to the sound of the television coming from the living room. He watched the news which gave more updates on what was happening with the new president and how he had "pardoned" Nixon and how angry people were over that including my father who threw a bag of potato chips at the television. Nixon, Nixon, he's our man, came an old song. Throw McGovern in the garbage can.

My father came in to say goodnight, kissed my forehead, told me to eat something if I woke up late, and then went into his bedroom. I waited an hour, in the dark, staring at the ceiling where the trees danced between my room and street lamps. Then I slipped out of bed, retrieved the tape reel, and soundlessly left the house.

The streets were like an abandoned movie set where all the arc lamps had been turned off and darkness had fallen on the carpentry. The cars lined up on the sidewalks were as silent as the dead houses. A comfortable wind had come in off the bay and was rustling the tree branches. I moved swiftly, the tape tucked under my shirt, my hand pressed over it to keep it from falling. No one saw me. I snuck across the avenue to the spot where Big Ben had clipped the chain on the gate. There was a new chain and a new lock, but I climbed over the fence and tumbled down the other side. I was in the forbidden zone, the dead land where the prisoners from the Island aimed their rubber boats during their watery escapes. I was never meant to have the voice on the tape, and I was never meant to be on this field at night. I was half a block from my home, but it was a world away.

I knew the ground so I needed little light, but I stumbled across a few dips in the soil, tripped over half-buried stones. I stayed clear of the mound of tall grass by the wooden bench where two summers earlier we had found a dead dog and watched it decay over several weeks. A cloud shrouded moon obscured my course, but I found my way around the first dugout and along the path that snaked in a semi-circle about the shore of the bay. The oil-stained water did not surf or crash against rocks. It lay limpid and still, except for the rustle of small creatures in the weeds along the banks.

I was heading for the large field behind all the diamonds, the landfill that had extended the area back out into the bay. From that vantage point, we had watched the airplanes landing and taking off, had spied the prison buildings on the Island, and had seen the ruins of the abandoned hospital on the far island where my grandmother said Typhoid Mary had spent her final days. In the dark of the cloudy night, this was a savage land, haunted by shrouds, shadowed by mysteries and headless entities. My fear of the reel I carried under my shirt was greater than my fear of those shrouds.

I didn't bring out the flashlight till I was at the mound, the same mound where Mike had wiped out on his bicycle when he tried to use the natural ascent of the soil as his daredevil cyclist take-off ramp. I knew that the land here was soft and that it came away in your hands like sand. I fell to my knees, turned on the flashlight and tilted it on the ground, then began to scoop out the dirt with small heaves.

I put the tape reel into the hole I had made, then began to push it all back. A shadow came across me and I fell to the side, kicking with my feet, perhaps crying out a bit. The shadow was larger than a man and it moved forward. I daringly raised the flashlight and saw him, like some dark ogre brought into being by fear itself. He lifted an arm against the light and said, "Fer Christ sakes, get that outta my eyes." The flashlight fell and he became a shadow once more.

A voice spoke out from the darkness. "What you doing back here, huh? You got nothing better to do? Come on, go home! Your father's going to be worried…"

"What do you care about my father?" I said loudly.

The shadow fell silent at my words. I could feel it staring at me. My face must have been catching some light from the street lamps that shone like distant beacons from the direction of the row homes. Then he said, "What's going on is none of your business."

"Why are the police after you?"

"You got some nerve."

"Where's your mother?"

He paused again, this time for longer than was comfortable. "She's back home, what you want with her? What you got there? You burying something?"

"I crashed my bike here. I'm looking for something I dropped."

"At eleven o'clock at night? Give me a break. You got some nerve, coming out here at night. Come on, I'll take you home."

He reached out his hand and for some reason I took it. It was hard, callused, and disturbingly warm. He pulled at me and I came off the ground, then he was walking me with one hand on my back. We walked along the path back toward the gate like a father and a son. I didn't know how I felt about that.

I told him: "All my friends are really upset."

"There's nothing to get upset about."

When we got to the gate there was a car waiting, the same black limo that had been there two weeks earlier. The gate was opened and two men were standing on the sidewalk. One of them waved a hand, "What's with the kid?"

"Don't mind him, he's alright. He's just confused. Go on, go home. Don't tell your father you was out this late. Go on." As I started off he called me back. He rubbed my head with one big paw. "You're ok, you know. Go to school and get educated. Don't get into trouble. "

After a paralyzed pause, I walked from the fence and started to cross the avenue. Not a car was in sight as if the neighborhood had been evacuated after the spread of a contagion. As I arrived on the sidewalk, I saw that Billy Delaware's garage door was closed and would probably remain so for the rest of the summer, perhaps forever. Billy Delaware who had fought in a war couldn't protect me against Big Ben. One of the men from the car grumbled, "How are we going to do this?" Then I was too far away to hear anything.

My mind went to the small mound in the rocky dirt by the wooden bench. The dog had been lying there supported by the mound, already rotten, full of insects and flies. The eyes had been gone and the face had been sagging to a sadness I could not comprehend. It was my first corpse and it had given me bad dreams until that moment that I walked away from Big Ben in the Manor night. The dog was now gone, the fear remained.

The night darkened, if that was even possible, and the clouds obscured even the faintest moonlight. The streetlamps guided me on my walk home, past the wooden fencing, by the police phone box on the post, over the cracks in the sidewalk squares. Somewhere in the dark sky, a late flight cut a line through the clouds on its way to the LaGuardia airport runways, carrying passengers from their cross-Atlantic flight, alerted to the news that somewhere out in the pitch of the night their destination was arriving. Taxis would be waiting to shuttle them to hotels and they would continue their much needed sleep through the Queens night.

Big Ben is gone now. So are many of my neighbors from the Manor. They are now all shadows from a buried dream. As many times as I hear the tapes in my head, the musings of Billy Delaware, the Italian opera, the car horns and airplane engines, or the mixed-up comic voices of some frightened children who were just trying to understand how a machine could speak in their own voices, they all remain forever gone, buried in the landfill like a wrathful mummy with no tongue, sharing a grave with the bones of a dead dog, trapped on the other side of some unopposed chasm that gently tells me to go home and not tell my father that I have been out late.

Atalanta's Run

1986. The Garden Bay hung like a dead weight around Justin Missal's spirit, until Atalanta Cosmopolis moved to Queens from Providence, RI. She arrived at Bryant High on a spring afternoon in the middle of math period while Justin was blocking out all attempts by a very flustered teacher to explain quadratic equations to his bored mind, choosing instead to stare at the sycamore branches that tapped against the classroom window like beckoning fingers trying to reveal a hidden pathway to a happier world.

"Boys, girls," came the familiar voice of Principal Silbert, rat-faced and half-blind, "this is Atalanta Cosmopolis. She's going to be joining us because her family just moved to New York."

Justin rotated, thinking quietly to himself, Atalanta. What a name! And when his head was fully turned, his ears gave way to the presidency of his chest, which was suddenly seized as if stepping into thick bog mud. The girl standing next to Silbert in front of the chalkboard was a tall, thick, dark-eyed, raven-haired girl, dressed in dirty blue jeans and a man's checkered flannel shirt. The only attempt at femininity was a barrette that clipped a bang of hair behind her left ear.

"Hi," she said, waving, almost reluctantly. "Hi."

Silbert beamed although it was doubtful he could see Atalanta very well. "Class, make sure that she feels welcome. She's a lovely girl and I'm sure you'll like her."

A few of the ruder boys made some even ruder noises and Silbert's face went dark, as if a light bulb had been switched off. Atalanta smiled slyly with one side of her face and cast a defiant look of self-sufficiency. She tugged at her book bag, which was slung over one shoulder, and slid into an empty seat near the back of the room. The teacher stepped back into the center of the room's composition and continued his futile talk about upside down parabolas.

After class, Justin followed the new girl to gym, abandoning her at the locker room door, which he almost walked through in his trance. As he changed into his shorts, he heard the voices around him in the boys' locker boisterously screaming their opinions:

"She's a butch! You see those arms on her?"

"I hope she takes up wrestling. I can't wait to tackle her!"

"Yeah, well just give me a week and I'll have her in the movie balcony."

"No way! She'll eat you alive. There'll be nothing left but your sneakers!"

Justin remained silent. He stared at his weedy body in the locker room mirror, thinking that he and Atalanta would make a strange looking couple. He was far from the paragon of Apollonian perfection. She would never be interested him. The more he thought about himself the more he had to hate: a miserable attachment to his mother; ugly birthmarks on his neck; a pale complexion which sunlight never darkened, only burned; his many phobias which included an irrational fear of deflated balloons, amongst others. Atalanta, on the other hand, looked strong and confident, ready to wrestle the world to its knees.

His suspicions were confirmed when he hit the floor of the gymnasium. The entire class was staring upwards at the running track that was elevated above the basketball hoops. Atalanta, her powerful legs churning the ground, was speeding along the curves like a crazed animal. Her dark hair flew behind her, her thick arms cut through the air with graceful arcs, her plump breasts heaved beneath her Bryant High gym shirt. From the floor, many cries of

"Holy Shit!" littered the air. The Bryant boys were awed, trapped in the presence of a terrible force they could not comprehend.

Even the gym instructor, a stocky woman in a jumpsuit, was speechless. No one moved from their position while Atalanta circled one lap after another. Then finally, after completing the track a dozen times, she emerged down the iron staircase, breathing heavy, pumping her arms, bouncing on her feet and spiraled through the air in a fabulous cartwheel that landed her before the parallel bars. Evidently, she was just getting started.

Justin lowered his face, thinking: I'm not going to win any points with her in looks or charm or personality. But I sure can run. Being chased by bigger kids my whole life has certainly put some fire in my legs.

Throughout each period after gym, he thought of Atalanta and her beckoning body, solid and rooted in the dark primal past where women were hunters and brutes and shed their monthly blood upon the earth to the sounds of pounding drums. They took men when they cared and deposited them where they wished; they ran the tribes, drove the chariots, tossed spears at the golden antelopes and were worshipped as goddesses because it was their loins that gave new life to the world. Justin, who previously had only pined after physically underdeveloped girls, small-chested button-cute nymphs, felt his adolescence rocked and his sexuality sabotaged.

After school in the courtyard, he gathered the nerve to approach Atalanta as she was waiting for the school bus. She seemed a bit hesitant at first to talk but Justin moved forward, fueled by faith in his secret plan.

"What's your name again?" Justin asked boldly, although he had repeated it back to himself a hundred times since gym.

"Atalanta." Her voice was low and gruff.

"That's like the coolest name I ever heard! What's your last name?"

"Cosmopolis."

"Isn't that that place in Greece…"

She rolled her eyes. "No, that's something else, you moron."

Justin felt like she had punched him. Her language was strong, like someone from the tough part of town. And she had called him a moron; that wasn't exactly the best way to open a relationship. He regrouped his thoughts and said, "I like the way you ran today."

"Yeah," she said.

"I don't suppose you want to race. I'm pretty fast."

Her eyes dismissed him with indifference. She's repulsed by me, Justin thought. He wavered, then asked, "Where did Silbert say you were from?"

She looked back at him and shrugged. "Providence, as in Rhode Island," she said.

"Yeah? Where in Providence?" His face was one big smile revealing crooked teeth.

"Right, like you really know that city?"

"Of course I do. I'm not some small town hick you know."

"Ok," she said. "Atwells Avenue. I lived in the tallest apartment building overlooking I-95. My father is a big fucking idiot who had his own company and he had to go get indicted by the government, so now we're living like damned gangsters on a witness protection program in this little shithole of a neighborhood!"

Justin kept a wide smile frozen on his face. "That's nice," he said.

"So what does your father do for a living?" she said snidely.

Justin shrugged. "Oh, a little of this and a little of that."

"Sounds like a big loser. Like that retard I have for a father. Is there anything to do in this town instead of going to school? I mean for fun." she asked.

Justin nodded. "Oh, we got lots of things. There's a miniature golf course where Billy Snyder sells pot and the candy store where you can get comic books. And a couple of years ago there was a shooting here, right where we're standing."

Atalanta's eyes clicked into place, drawn like a bird to a branch by his words. "Shooting?"

"My cousin went nuts and shot up the place, and then he killed himself."

"And that happened right here?"

"Yeah, I was going to write a magazine article about it."

She looked around at the line of London planetrees lining the main drag. "I hope something like that happens again. I got lots of energy just pumping. I need some action, you know what I mean? You want to run? Meet me over in Astoria Park at 5 o'clock. And be prepared to lose!"

Justin nodded. She turned and sprinted off, dismissing the bus that had just pulled up to the bus stop. Justin dropped his smile and realized just how sore his facial muscles had become from holding that pose.

Justin walked home almost as a challenge to compete with his Providence girl. He followed Hazen Street to the entrance to the Rikers Island Bridge. "I've seen pictures of Providence," he said proudly, "and this is far more beautiful!"

He got home at three-thirty, nervous and excited. From the smell, he knew his mother was cooking his favorite pot pie dinner. His father, as usual, was slumped on the couch, snoring, still in his security uniform, his night job hours in the future. Justin bounded into his room, seeing it as if for the first time. The science fiction posters, the three-foot tall stuffed Snoopy, the cardboard box of Marvel Comics, they would all have to go, spiraled into his closest to make way for a more mature and adult-like room fit to receive a classy girl whose father had owned his own business. He looked longingly at the bed, with its cowboy bed sheets, ready to accommodate his first woman. On these sheets they would discover new worlds, learn new ways of being. He felt like it was only hours away.

His mother, bored and half-asleep, gave him his pot pie. "What are you grinning about?" she asked.

"I think I'm in love," he confessed, poking his fork through the browned crust.

"God help us," his mother groaned.

"What's that supposed to mean, Ma? Where's the support? You're supposed to be happy for me."

"You're not fit to be in love," she snapped. "Who is this girl anyway?"

"Atalanta Cosmopolis!" he said, proudly.

His mother took a step backwards. "Cosmopolis? What are you getting messed up with that for? I heard about her criminal father."

"What do you mean?"

"You stay away from that girl. She's killed people."

"Who? What?"

"And they say she hunts bears. She goes to Maine and she hunts down bears in the woods. You want to date a girl who kills bears? You're crazy."

"Ma, I respect you and everything. But I can take her! I'm strong, too!" He held up a spindly arm for her to inspect.

"What the hell are you talking about? That Cosmopolis girl is bad news. They're Greek, you know. They live over near the deaf school."

"What does being Greek have to do with anything? Her father had his own company. Maybe they have some money left. That'll please you, wouldn't it? If I marry into that?"

"I need mob money like I need a hole in the head," she barked. And then she abandoned her son to his dinner.

Mob, he thought. But they're *Greek*.

The East River cooled as the sun turned crimson, shining between the budding spring trees. Justin arrived at the park and wryly nodded toward the three used condoms that were strewn about the willow trees. Apparently, there were others in his school who were bored with quadratics.

He sprinted along the edge of the branch, his legs pumping, his arms dodging the air. For the first time he noticed that his ankles were so thin that his sneakers looked like white cement blocks on the end of stalks. He stood for a moment contemplating his dilemma, thinking of the way Atalanta's thigh muscles had flexed on the track, the way her breasts had revealed their voluptuous violence through her shirt, and the barrette over her left ear that had excited him as much as any other feature because of its innocence, its attempt at decoration, like a factory courtyard placing a vase of flowers on an iron pedestal.

"Ready to rumble?" Her voice came from over his shoulder and he squeaked like a girl. His hand shot to his mouth but the sound had already escaped into the air.

"Who?" he said, and spun about. She was standing under a weeping willow, the thin fingers of the tree barely brushing her rough face. She wore a cutaway heavy metal T-shirt (he didn't recognize the band) and thin blue running pants through which her legs emerged like pylons plugging the earth. Her heavy chest heaved with her breaths, as if she had run all the way from 77th Street without stopping and she was just getting cranked up.

"You can't conquer me," she said bluntly.

"I don't want to conquer you," he said. "I want to race you. I have to feel your power beside me."

She laughed, a peculiar arrogant laugh that didn't move many muscles on her face. "No, I mean you can't conquer me! You get me?"

"Tough Rhody girl," he said.

"Damn right."

"Then if you're so tough, how come your daddy's chased by the government."

"Because he's a fucking moron, like you!" she howled, and yanked at the willow, pulling down several branches in a flurry of foliage. "I got to live out here now, in this backwater tank taking shit from creeps like you!"

Justin felt his courage flee. He crumpled like a collapsible chair and sat on a rock, a little folded stick insect. "Ok," he said.

She moved forward toward him and he held up his arms, like he was expecting her to eat him alive. Surprisingly, she sat down next to him and sighed. A long pause ensued during which Justin held his breath, like some space traveler who has arrived at a fresh planet and is awaiting the analysis of the possibly poisoned air.

Eventually, Atalanta put two finger tips on his right shoulder. It was the first female contact he had experienced since his mother last changed his diaper a long time ago. He shuddered, felt a stirring in his loins.

"You listen," she commanded. "I like you. I mean, I'm starting to respect you. I know you're just some goofy hick but you got balls, you know. You come out here looking like some fucking dweeb challenging me to some kind of race when you know and I know that you couldn't possibly beat me...and for what? Because you want to see my legs! Well, here they are!" She slapped one leg and then grabbed his hand and put his palm down on her hard thigh. "Feel all you want! I don't give a shit! You're never going to own me."

His hand was on her thigh. He lost all track of time and spatial coordinates. When he curled his fingertips, he felt the softness of her skin over the muscle. His mind spun into some vortex where he was starting to forget even his own name.

"Yes, I am," he said,

"What?" she asked.

"I will own you!"

She openly laughed in his face. He felt a blast of onion and peppers from her mouth. "What the hell is that supposed to mean!"

He took his hand reluctantly from her leg and pointed toward a tree far across the field, in the direction of the Hell Gate Bridge. "See that oak tree over there. We're going to race. And if I win, then you have to date me for a month."

"What?"

"I mean it."

"But you're not going to win?"

"Then you shouldn't be afraid to make the deal."

"This is crazy!"

"Come on, let's shake on it."

"What? That I have to date you for a month if you beat me?"

"Yeah, that's fair, isn't it?"

She sat and pondered, her face hardening as the sun lowered toward Long Island City where the factories were just starting to blow their 5:30 sirens. After an intolerable pause, she looked up at Justin and said boldly, "You got a deal," and thrust her hand into his. Then she leaned forward and hugged him. He didn't remember much about the hug except for feeling her chest, a sensation that reminded him of jump starting a car with alligator clips. He felt new life injected into him through her comforting breasts.

"What a rail you are," she said in return, pinching his bicep, then took off toward the edge of the willow tree where the field began; the long run to the oak tree lay before them like the beckoning pylon of paradise.

Atalanta Cosmopolis hunted bears, this was true. A friend of her father's, who she would not sleep with, a Wall Street trader who is now in jail, knew of trails up in Maine where they could seclude themselves for days tracing the spoors of Benjamin Bear, the mythical creature blown out of proportion through years of girlhood fantasy and campfire legends. Whether Benjamin Bear really was over ten feet tall on his clawed feet, or whether he ate five tourists a season, were facts that could not reasonably be verified, but Mr. Marx — who Atalanta nicknamed Groucho, worked on Wall Street and made millions of dollars a year and wanted so much to have sex with Atalanta Cosmopolis, his strategic business partner's primal pagan witch of a daughter — claimed to have once seen Ben the Bear during a wood hike with his son's ten year old scouting troop.

"Savage as the worst nightmare conjured from the darkest place on earth," he would remember. "He came out of the forest, a black mountain shifting under the canopy of night stars, his nostrils flaring in the upwind of fifteen young boys and one sweaty man and the smoky remains of a camp fire. I awoke, grabbed my rifle, saw the pitch black shift upwards, tower against the tree line, and open its eyes that shone like beams in the darkness, these two pits through which I saw death crying for our lives."

To Atalanta this was just the shit. She begged Groucho to take her hunting, to bring her to that snowy region where the trees connect the earth and the sky, where man lives by his body and his wits alone, where nature works its unpredictable patterns and plays havoc with the man-made script. Mr. Cosmopolis, sequestered behind his cell phones and his law suits, basically waved a hand and said, "Yeah, whatever. Just get him to sign this piece of paper. Blow him if you have to, but don't come back with that paper unsigned, you hear me."

Groucho did do her the courtesy of bringing two tents, but he kept her out by the campfire till long after midnight. He insisted on reading her a poem that he had just written before leaving New

York: "A woman is like the vast night sky, infinite in spirit yet confined by the horizon, steeped in mystery, witness to all events that transpire upon the earth yet always silent, host to strange nocturnal creatures, mother to the powdery rock that lights the darkness of man, both friend and foe to the woodsman at end of day, who seeks to find his lonely way home."

She couldn't help but cry, not because she found his poem so romantic or moving, but because she thought him painfully obvious and pathetic. She left him to stew in his own mundanity and slept a cautious night in her tent.

That weekend, Atalanta never saw Benjamin Bear, but she did bag a bear half the size of the mythical beast. Another party of trashy beer-bellied real estate salesmen on their summer vacation was also tracking the bear and had compromised the spoor trails. When they saw Atalanta emerge from the trees, her breasts pushing past the flaps of her khaki vest, her handsome face framed by her bangs of jet-black hair, they stopped shouting like idiots, took several steps back, and stared at her long and hard. She raised her rifle in a mock gesture of conquest, then motioned for Groucho to emerge from his place in the trees, his face red with rage. Atalanta screamed and shook her weapon until the real estate men took off down the mountain and disappeared.

"Ben's going to know we were disorganized," Groucho said. "He doesn't care about any difference between us and them. We have to earn back his respect."

But Ben had summoned the little bear, the one that only stood six foot when it stood on its clawed feet and wasn't known to have eaten any tourists that season, as some form of gracious offering. Appease the Goddess, sacrifice the young to encourage her to remove danger for another year. Atlanta had the impression that she was being worshipped even by this bear that terrified her.

They saw it at dawn, gnawing at a tree trying to get at the gum. It sniffed the air, turned its pelted body toward the south, and humped down the incline toward the safety of the caves.

"We'll follow it that far," Groucho said. "Follow my foot falls."

They crept down the incline till they could see the clearing and the gaping holes against the rocks. The bear had not yet entered its shelter, its eyes looking back, sad and lonely on either end of its flaring wet nose. Atalanta, at her leader's prompting, positioned herself behind the forward incline of a mammoth oak, her knees hard against the moist lichen, her left elbow supporting her heaviness while her hands lifted the hard metal of her rifle to eye-level. In the scope she could see the youthful hairy face, the marble eyes, the twitching nose, the tight mouth.

There was a whisper in her ear: "You've earned his respect."

Then she fired. It was her first kill, and Groucho took her down to the body and they cut it with a machete and she smeared the blood on her cheeks just as she had read about in books on Indians. They stood over the body and hugged each other, resisting a moment's temptation to make love in the puddle of bear's blood. It was then that they heard the forest, dark and deep, laughing at them from afar, and pulled apart.

"What the crap was that?" Groucho said. When five minutes of silence passed and they felt comfortable enough to talk again, he handed her the machete and told her that she could castrate her kill. He also produced a leather pouch.

They exited the woods on the fifth day not having seen Benjamin Bear, but Atalanta was convinced that they had heard him laugh, that somewhere in the forest he was watching and approving of their slaughter, that some lesser bear of no significance to his kin had made the ultimate sacrifice to maintain the balance between the forest, the bear kind, and the bipeds that came into the woods with their beer bottles and deadly fire sticks.

Justin didn't remember the start of the race, had no memory of whether they had decided to run on 'three' or there was some general signal that initiated their sprint. He just knew that he was running and that from the very start, his lungs burned like some ember was glowing in their spongy depths. His concrete blocks for feet pumped hard against the ground.

He could smell her by his side, cared little to look sideways for verification, fearing that it would slow him down, that he needed to be hell-bent upon the oak. But he smelled the onions and peppers from her most recent meal wafting into the air, probably escaping from her mouth as she pumped the oxygen in and out of her chest. He could swear he could also feel the thuds of her heels against the hard earth under his own feet.

He didn't look sideways, but he inadvertently looked down, noticing that the ground beneath him was a savage mix of grass, brown weeds, compacted soil, cracked soda cup lids, torn pages from magazines and newspapers, crumbled wrappers, slivers of broken glass, shards of metal, rusted nails and lost keys. It was industrial land, cluttered and beautiful, land that he had grown up on. He had never known any other.

Atalanta was perpetually by his side. As the oak tree grew perceptibly larger, he felt he couldn't shake her. Her breathing wasn't even labored like his, but steady and hardly audible. She had powerful lungs and years of training, he figured.

He knew he had a plan, and it was a wild desperate one. He had devised it while standing in the gymnasium watching her run the track. It was something that came to him from his childhood when his mother claimed to be psychic. She boasted that she could summon the frogs, by standing on her front steps and making a peculiar clacking sound with her throat, one that originated in a deep throat gulp and ended with a popping of the lips with a sharp crack in between. She once had taken him out to the steps and shown him how that funny noise could bring at least one or two bullfrogs up out of the muddy bay near their home and stand on the concrete of their front steps and stare at them with those bulbous eyes. Justin had spent his entire childhood trying to imitate that noise, and once, only once, when he was in middle school, he stood on the steps in the evening gloom and clacked for five minutes until an ugly old bullfrog leapt up to meet him, stared at him, blinked, turned its eyes in four directions, then leapt back into the darkness from which it had emerged. Justin knew that he had the power in him. If he had done it once, he could do it again.

As they ran, he struggled with his breath to give him the stamina to clack. It came from his mouth like a hoarse cry for help. He even took the time to turn and watch Atalanta for three seconds. He saw her large body moving against gravity, perpetually suspended in the air as she sped, seemingly along the tops of the tallest grass. He knew she couldn't possibly be levitating, but her legs were pumping with the arcing grace of beautiful music. It was as if he were seeing her in slow motion. She did not look back; her face was focused on the oak tree, as if the tree had the gravitational pull that was propelling her forward. Justin continued to clack.

Halfway across the field. No frogs. Feeling foolish Justin closed his eyes and focused on the pain in his legs. He shouldn't have sprinted from his home to the park, should have saved his stamina. He resisted the temptation to fall upon the ground and become a heaving, gasping bundle of sticks and pumping lungs.

What was at stake? Atalanta? This beautiful Greek girl with her Eastern Europe mysteries, her dark skin, her Rhody swagger, her bear killing lustiness, this fleeting pagan who ran beside him in some desperate race to avoid having to date Justin Missal. He yearned for her, wanted to share in her energies and her strength. He wanted to be more than Justin, he wanted to be the mate of this wilderness creature that no gym teacher could tame.

His legs still ran but his mind knew that he had failed. The tree was getting closer, but Atalanta was ahead, and he couldn't possibly catch up. His heart was hurting as much as his lungs and he felt a deep sorrow, as if a life's goal had been derailed from the tracks of possibility. He surrendered to humiliation, began to plan his concession speech, even more importantly contemplated racing past the oak tree, across 20th Ave., down Hazen Street until he arrived back at his house, only to collapse in his bed and never set foot into daylight again. Atalanta Cosmopolis had destroyed him and he, himself, had been the engine of that destruction.

The thought that burned through his mind: I am no Apollo. I am not from the Sun. I do not cast golden apples from the chariot I drive across the sky to the women of the Earth.

It was just then that the impossible happened.

She raced to prove to Justin that she did not desire him. He was just another conquest on that crooked path on which she walked through life. Like Groucho who had been her teacher in the art of death, Justin the fleet-footed dork would be her student in the art of life. As she bolted from the starting line at the edge of the industrial meadow, she knew that he was in for a hard ride, for she barely felt the exertion, and even at the start of the race he was heaving like an asthmatic. She needn't have to summon confidence, or challenge herself, or even run faster than what was natural for her. Justin Missal's boasts were all hot air; already he was limping along like an amateur.

She had never had any problems outwitting men, young or old. The young especially were easily confused, for they thought almost entirely in terms of sexual conquest, which painfully few of them were even barely adequate at, and never with her; the older men, Groucho included, differed only in terms of time span. They moved glacially, setting up scenarios, situations and chance meetings way in advance, knowing that successfully obtaining a woman, especially a clever one, was something that could take weeks, even years. Their aims were identical, but they had the ability to delay short term satisfaction, except occasionally when they were drunk.

So Atalanta ran casually, taking her long strides, confident that the stick legged boy who bounded beside her was inconsequential, that before long the ridiculous challenge would be over and he would just fade back into the gymnasium crowd, one more boy with protruding shorts watching her round the track curves and go home to touch themselves and dream about her. She even considered the embarrassment of being seen running with him, as if this race were some sort of tacit agreement to be friendly. She only hoped that those who witnessed from Shore Blvd. or even from the knoll past the bridge, would also witness her victory, to see her touch base with the oak tree and turn to receive her losing opponent with a massive slug to the jaw with one of her large hands. She wanted to leave the park with Justin flat on his back, his big sneakers facing skywards, his rattled head lying amidst the discarded candy wrappers and rusted soda cans. That image concluded all her fantasies.

A third of the way across the field the moron started making these little clucking noises with his mouth. It was weird, like some sort of bipedal insect was racing beside her. Was it a grotesque nervous habit that happened when he was scared or under stress?

Perhaps he was even trying to distract her from her course, which would be typical of such a clod. She turned to look at him, briefly, a fleeting second, enough to see his reddened face, his grasping arms swinging through the air like a fan belt snapped on a running motor, his legs skipping up with his knobby knees practically hitting his sunken chest. But to her surprise, he was close. She was only ahead by about a foot. If the silly boy had some fuel left in reserve, if he somehow managed to pull off a final sprint, she was actually in trouble – not of losing: she was confident of ultimate victory; but of not having the time to turn and prepare herself for the final punch. She would need a good six or seven feet of distance to pull that one off.

Time to move forward, she thought, and sped up her engines. There was plenty of juice left in her, and she was soon a good two feet ahead. She heard him whimper, a typical reaction of a pathetic boy on the verge of realizing that he is not the alpha male of his tribe, that the women warriors have stepped in to reclaim their rightful thrones. What dreams must be breaking, what delusions must be evaporating from this miserable boy's mind.

She saw the tree enlarging, like she was hoisted as a maidenhead on the cowcatcher of a locomotive moving perpetually onwards. The goal was a few dozen feet away and she hadn't even taken ten breaths since the start of the race. This inane man-child, this spindly joke, would have to have favor from the gods to...

Her eyes had fallen from the tree to the ground. She had been watching the compacted soil race beneath her. The crushed soda cans, the paper straw sheaths, metal shards and scraps of paper... all beneath her. Then suddenly, without warning, thrust up from the soil like a gestating child, a single piece of fruit, an apple in fact, golden and shiny. Thinking quickly, not even contemplating what strange effect was at hand, she bent to scoop it up, slowing considerably and feeling Justin breeze past her as she got back to her running stance. She lost a little extra time staring down at the fruit, marveling at its clear golden skin, its shine and luster. But she soon realized that Justin was ahead by a few feet and she sprinted forward, quickly catching up.

What was this possibly about? Her mind was awhirl with

explanations, none the least of which was genetic mutation. But isn't it true that apples grow from trees? And she had never heard of a golden one. Then suddenly there was another one, beneath her, and she stooped to scoop it up. It was as beautiful as the first, even more so. She slowed to a trot and took a bite into the first one she had plucked from the ground. It was heavenly sweet, and juice ran down her lips.

The taste was so beautiful that she stopped completely and stared around for more. There was a third, peering from behind a flapping piece of newspaper that was caught on some tall weeds. She chewed and swallowed another bite from the first while she strolled to the third. She plucked it and examined it, noting the same elegance and beauty of form and color. Then she realized that she was winded, that the race had taken more from her than she had realized.

The apples were so beautiful, so magnificent, that she hadn't even noticed that she stood about ten feet from the oak tree where Justin lay like a slug, his feet splayed in the field, his chest heaving like he were having a seizure, his face bloated and mouth agape, trying to drink in the precious air that seemed to elude his lungs, and one hand, the fingers spread, pressed against the tree trunk, straining to maintain its contact with the bark as if his life depended on it.

"I won!" he said with great exertion.

Atalanta, shiny with sweat, her thighs beautiful and huge in the reddening glow from the descending sun, stood staring at her apples which she extended before her like trophies of some Olympian contest.

Justin didn't get to his feet before Atalanta joined him at the oak tree. She was dark and silhouetted against the sun, which was almost now behind the factories. He was afraid of her, terrified. With the last bits of breath he could muster from his chest, he started making his mother's clacking sounds. He was still hoping for the miracle.

Atalanta came down gracefully, slid in beside him, nestled her large body against his tiny frame, rolled to her side and pressed her heavy breasts into his back. Then she put a single finger tip on his lips and made a shushing noise. He was stunned by the feel of her flesh and her heat.

"I won," he said.

"Yes," she said. "I know." And she reached out her arm, her hand holding one of the golden apples, and held it before his face.

He stared at it like it was an alien artifact. "What?" he said.

She leaned forward and kissed his ear, wetting it ever so gently. His shoulder came up instinctively. "That tickles," he said, giggling. Then she whispered, slightly, barely audible, in a tender voice that discarded her gruffness: "I am offering you the treasure from heaven. The goddess of love is speaking to us. Eat."

He paused, then took the apple, bit into it. It was sweet and nice. When it hit his stomach, it made him feel strong and confident. Then he felt her breasts against his back and one of her hands resting warmly on his rib cage, and he turned his whole body around so he was facing her. They lay against each other, their faces inches apart. Her face was huge, a wall of beauty and mystery. He felt so small against her.

They rested for an hour. At some point they fell asleep. No one saw them in their bower, lovers in spirit if not in deed, children of heaven under their eternal tree.

The sun was down when they awoke. They got to their feet, stretched, stared at each other, smiled with great embarrassment.

He spoke first. "I know I won and everything, but you don't have to date me. I'm sorry about all that."

She smiled. "Friends," she said, and held out her hand. They shook and then she said, "You're ok, you know. I'm sorry I called you a moron."

"Thank you," he said.

They looked around for the apples and to their disappointment couldn't find them. They had vanished without a trace.

"Oh, well," he said.

He walked her home all the way to 77th. They walked across a grass enclosure where an old house had burned down and stopped to look at the ruins, only the foundation left. They confessed to each other that they both liked ruins, and Atalanta said that one day they should go to Greece together and look at all the old stuff. She said that he would like Greece because the family had a big yacht called the Argo that they could travel around in. "It's pretty cool," she said.

Her house was a pleasant center hall Colonial that looked like it had cost a good deal of money. He turned to her and asked, "You're not really in a witness protection program, are you?"

She shrugged. "There are certain people you don't fuck with, you know."

Her father appeared on the porch, a grim faced man with one eyebrow and a piercing stare. "Who is this young man?" he said.

"This is Justin," Atalanta said quickly.

The father furrowed his brow. "Just don't get her pregnant," he said and vanished into the house again.

Justin kissed her on the cheek and said goodbye, then walked back to his own home. His father was just getting up to go to work, his mother had finished all the dishes, and the sun was fully hidden in the underworld. He went to his room both confused and elated, opened his math textbook, looked at the quadratics and binomial expansions and thought of Greece and heavy women's bodies and golden apples and a chariot drawing its way across the sky, carrying the sun in all its brilliance.

Garden Bay Vignettes

The Manor Lounge—
Old Man Clifford

Clifford Brattle was a ghostly presence at the Manor Lounge. He trailed behind him the shadowy wisps of his brother John who had died on the beaches at Normandy. Unwisely, he had spent twenty years talking about the event until everyone in the Manor's only watering hole knew the story of the Omaha landing from a man who had not been present at the event and whose brother had been machine gunned as soon as his landing platform hit the sand.

But he rarely talked about it now, having learned his lesson from alienating too many people, finally coming to accept the depressing effect he was having, and sat under the over-hanging television set with his endless stream of Budweiser, staring at the oak wall paneling like the wood grains were ciphers revealing some palliative of truth.

He was well into his fifties, his head almost completely gray, and bore about him the dull sadness of some aborted life, cut short before he had the chance to experience any of the petty joys he saw around in others. He had never married, never had children or nephews or nieces, and never had much of an income from his fifteen years of working odd jobs at LaGuardia and in the neighborhood. For the teenagers of the Manor, he was remembered from their childhood as the slow-witted man in the dark green jumpsuit who was often seen dragging vacuums and toolboxes in and out of the boiler rooms that lined the backyards, haunting utility hallways at the airport, smoking on breaks at the candy store lunch counters. Once he even had a janitor's position at the public school but was unceremoniously fired for reasons that were never made clear.

He was Old Man Clifford before his time and often spoke of how the land was cleaner and smelled better before "that fat mayor" put in the airport. He had already seen two pivotal turning points in history come and go over the neighborhood: the building of the Grand Central Parkway and the Garden Bay Manor itself, which sloped down toward Bowery Bay and the large slabs of airport runways and the bridge to the prison island. The neighborhood, with its cluster of attached two-family homes, once warm and welcoming with their pseudo-Tudor facades and enclosed courtyards, now grim with broken fences and dank cellar pits, where children played on the limbs of cracked and drying trees. The constant sound of airplanes landing and taking off from the runways with their Dopplerian delays and abrupt bursts colored the neighborhood with transient energy. So did the years, which came and went so quickly, leaving nothing behind but a sense of wasted days. The presence of so many children playing in the backyards and cellar pits, riding their bikes through the crowded streets amidst the Fords and Studebakers and other remnants of the 1950s did little to brighten Clifford's sense of new life being injected into an aborted attempt at the old one, now as dead as his D-Day brother, repeated often in legend and myth only for the purpose of manifesting the obvious: that life had ended on June 6, 1944. All else was memory.

Clifford sat with his beer, nursing the foam at the mug lip, tapping his loafers against the bar rail like a sullen Andy Capp. The bartender, Ricky, a young barrel chested boy who had grown up in Astoria, wiped the old man's spill from around his coaster with an alcohol-stinking rag.

"How's your mother?" he asked.

"Yep," was the reply. "Getting better."

"You still bringing her to that Ditmars doctor?"

"Hasn't killed her yet," he said.

The afternoon was disappearing, but the patrons of the Manor Lounge wouldn't have known. They lived in a perpetual shadow of the dark interior of their drinking hole. Brattle usually sat on a cracked red leather seat near the back phone booths, minding his business, dressed in his airport maintenance crew overalls and dark green cap, long into the mid-evening when he would, usually about nine o'clock, slide off the seat and take off down the avenue toward the row houses, one of them being where he lived with his mother, and vanish for the night. As the years went on he became more and more uncommunicative, although he was prone, when encouraged by an understanding friend, to wind up his story machine and belt out something that folks had all heard before. He was tolerated simply because he was the closest that the neighborhood came to having their own mythologizer.

"Too bad he never became a poet," Ricky always said. "He would have left here a long time ago to some New England college and sixteen years later some long obnoxious novel would come out with his name on it and all of us inside of it."

But he never became a poet. He became a drunk. Although no one ever really saw him drunk, except when he'd walk home on unsteady legs and think hard before replying to a question. He never collapsed or ran his mouth off in an inebriated rage of bitter discontent. No one ever saw him angry, but instead melancholic, filled with a heavy sadness that never expressed itself except in subtle tones of dialogue or his choice of subject matter, which tended toward morbidity. This evening he was seated next to Mike Pantios.

"Anything going on at the airport?" Mike said.

Brattle nodded. "People going to Florida, coming in from Los Angeles."

"You never got much chance to travel there, eh? I mean, it's ironic, you working at the airport."

"Nope."

Brattle coveted his drink, then closed his eyes as if trying to summon some interior power. Then he wagged a finger at Pantios. "The Yarrow boy's colored girl came in."

"What?"

"The Yarrow boy's got a colored girl. She came in from California and he met her there."

"Really," Mike nodded. "Is she good looking?"

"That's not the point. I don't care much for colored girls, but Yarrow met her when he was at school and now they're living together on Hazen Street." Brattle poured back into his drink as if either negating what he had just said, reflexively withdrawing from the responsibility of what he had put out, or merely pausing for dramatic effect, allowing his pronouncement in its stark plainness to stand for itself in the dusty air of the saloon.

Mike blew through his lips. "You have a problem with that Cliff? I mean we live in enlightened times and all."

"Wouldn't happen before," Brattle said, peering upwards. "A colored girl shouldn't be at a school like that."

"Well," Mike smirked, wiping the bar with his rag. "We just got a difference of opinion there, Cliff. Maybe because I'm younger than you or something...and I'm not a lefty or anything, but I got more respect for blacks than you have, you know. I don't mean any disrespect for you or anything, but I see things different."

"I don't mind coloreds," Brattle muttered. "I'm not a racist, if that's what you mean."

"I'm not calling you a racist, I know you're not a racist."

"I just have some proud ideas about marriage, is all."

"Yes, I understand Cliff. You want another one?"

Brattle tapped the bar and invoked another mug still foaming. He sat for another half-hour watching the ballgame progress, staring at the pixeled screen with a prolonged indifference. He never talked sports or even commented on any of the games he watched, but he seemed drawn to them, as if he was compelled to follow their internal logic of suspended tension and release, taking some silent delight in the orgasmic burst of the home run and the clearing of the bases regardless of who swung the bat or who ran to home or what number they wore on their backs or what emblem decorated their caps.

Ricky attempted to draw conversation from the game. "You got your bets on anyone, Cliff?" It was a Yankees-Indians game out of Cleveland and the other patrons at the bar were watching in semi-inebriated silence broken by occasional mutterings about records, batting averages, which kids were good, and dimly remembered games from a decade when the game was unpolluted by crass commercialism and junk food ads. Brattle leaned his face toward Ricky.

"You got your bets?" Ricky repeated.

"Nah," Brattle said. "I don't take sides."

"So I see."

Brattle sulked in silence for a moment. "I stopped taking sides a few years back, it never did me any good."

"Lost a lot of bets?"

"Bets? I never bet. I lived twice as long as you and I was here when a whole different game was going on. These streets aren't new, you know."

"I know Cliff, I'm just trying to make conversation."

"You think it's easy to see the airport get thrown down, all that concrete and the slabs. You think it's easy to watch the housing projects go up?"

"No, I never said it was."

"I don't care what clapboard house you were born in, I was born here in a house that got plowed under the parkway."

"I know Cliff."

Brattle threw a few bills on the bar and moved off his stool. Ricky remained silent as the older man floated past the jukebox and the circular tables void of customers and became a bleak shadow in the dull sunlight of the front door. The cars on the avenue were moving solemnly, dimly glimpsed residents of an alternative world.

"Bye Cliff," Ricky said picking up the money.

The streets curved toward the Bay, long canyons flanked by rows of attached homes. The commuters were all home for the evening and the television lights were flickering in the open windows. Brattle walked solemnly past the familiar doorways with their bright red paint and black numbers nailed slantwise on the wood, past the garbage bins lowered into the earth with their foot pedals and flip top lids.

Brattle felt an itching in his anus and knew that he wouldn't make it home in time. He glanced around for a place he could use, a bush, a fence. There was a paved walkway into an inner courtyard where some kiddie swings rested calmly in the windless air. He moved into the yard and noticed too late that some children were playing on the see-saws who hadn't been visible from the street. He moved to the far corner of the yard where a bush obscured most of his legs. After lowering his pants and squatting, he saw the children had halted in their tracks and were staring at him, frightened and confused.

"Damn them anyway," he figured and dumped his load onto the hard grassless dirt. He shuffled up his pants and moved away. By the time he had reached the street, he dared to look back. The children had moved over to the rubber matting under the swings and were staring at him. They jerked a bit as he glanced back, as if considering bolting, but remained still. Just another strike against him, he thought. Wouldn't do much to improve his reputation.

He shouted, "What'd you want me to do? Go in my pants?" They couldn't understand what it was like, when your body starts fighting you, mocking you with illness and promised death. They were still young and pliable. They could take falls and stay healthy on junk food.

There had been Mrs. Grace, the crazy one. Once, under a similar sky in a graying evening, she walked out onto the dirt road with no clothes, just a parasol over her head. She'd walk until her horrified son would come running with a shawl, his face stained with shame. Mrs. Grace was misshapen, lumpy, with flat hanging breasts. No child on that road took any delight in her madness.

Brattle came to the lamppost. It was at the corner of Hazen Street and 21st Avenue, just by the entrance to the bridge to Riker's Island. The guards were at their post but paying no mind to his direction, and the hot dog van that usually sat nearby had left for the evening, so he took his trembling fingers and touched the cold metal. Immediately he started to hear the voices.

"John in there?" he asked.

Just a confused jumble of hushed whisperings, angry barks of indistinguishable syllables and dull mewling. Suddenly, a haunted female saying, "Never in these years have I fashioned truth from your mouth. You must forgive the man who blinks."

Brattle nodded and broke the connection. He stared at the lamppost with an angry defiance. It had broadcast something that would confuse him for days. Those messages always meant something in the end, revealing their internal logic only in time with the passing of future events.

He had hoped for his brother. It was four weeks since he last heard John's deep toned voice vibrating through the inner wiring of the post: "My blood is in the sands." The message had come suddenly when Brattle leaned against the post to support his drunken legs. The voice was as sharp as a deeply ingrained memory revealed on a persistent magnetic tape. John Brattle was talking through the lamppost.

Each evening he tried to touch it again, hoping not to be seen by the guards on the bridge. Some nights he passed by without incident because the guards, having little to do with their time, watched him as he crawled furtively along the cyclone fencing. Other times they ignored him and he snuck a feel on the shiny grey metal.

He watched the guards at the security hut and imagined what it would be like if he walked toward them with a dumb smile on his face, just a crazy grin, the craziest he could conjure, his eyes shooting all sorts of insane suggestions. No, he thought, that wouldn't be threatening enough. Not in this day and age. I need something that a German machine gun would respond to.

He reached a hand into his jacket and felt for the pocket he had created with cloth and some sewing thread. That's where he kept his pistol, the little small caliber machine he had been carrying around with him for several years. It felt cold to the touch, but he knew it would heat up if he fired it. And if he walked toward the guards with his face frozen in a crazy rictus of a smile, the pistol exposed and thrust forward in one lumpy fist, he would assure his own end. The guards would bring forth their service revolvers and gun him down to save their own sorry lives. He knew they would do this, but he didn't feel ready for it yet.

One guard, the black one, the one he wanted to kill, waved to him.

"He doesn't know me," Clifford murmured, not even realizing that once you have been contemplating murdering a man, that man does indeed know you.

He grumbled and walked along the cyclone fencing toward the Yarrow house at the edge of the Bay.

Steinway Street— Gorilla Girl

Little Terrance saw the young woman step on the bus and stared owl-eyed while the bus pulled away from the stop; then he starting crying. He grabbed my coat and then pressed himself against me, crying so hard I feared he might start screaming. I pulled him up onto the concrete steps of the elevator factory and held him.

"That's the Gorilla Girl," he said, and begged me to take him home.

I had promised his mother I'd take him to the toy store, but we never got on the bus. Once he saw the Gorilla Girl he couldn't do it. The vehicle had been tainted with a menace and I knew that he would never set foot on it again, even if it meant missing trips to Steinway Street. I calmed him down and then walked him back to the Manor, along the cyclone fencing by the little league field, and crossed over the avenue, looking out for cars. Overhead a passenger plane circled on its way to the airport runways across the Bay and Terrance, who had been born under the flight paths and knew the roar of the engines from his very first days, now looked upwards with a dread that was nightmarish.

"It's just planes," I told him. "Come on."

His body trembled as we approached the row houses facing the Bay. He lived in the center court, and his kitchen window faced the walkways. His mother spotted us and ran outside, knelt down and wiped his face, half-laughing at his fright. She thanked me for trying and took him inside, leaving me on the street to ponder the significance of the Gorilla Girl.

I was fourteen years old and Maria was eighteen, but I knew her. Our street of row homes curved away from the Bay where the old Dutch farmhouse was and followed what had been the colonial post road around the corner and up to what we called the handball court, a concrete wall that had been cut into the hill so it wouldn't have to be leveled. The clapboard houses on top could be accessed by steep concrete stairs and many a time I witnessed the residents carrying their bags of groceries, two at a time, from their parked cars to their lofty perches. The view up there must have been grand; they could probably see all the way across the Bay to the prison island and the airport runways on the other side.

The white concrete wall wasn't meant for handball. There was parallel parking right in front, but when the cars were gone we used it to play handball anyway. None of us had ever been up in those homes. They existed in another world, the 1940s, before any of the Manor had been there. The people who lived up there may as well have been in another country, but many times Maria's mother had yelled down for us to stop making so much noise. She had an Italian accent and often the scent of garlic drifted down to the street, making our stomachs ache for pasta and tomatoes.

Maria was slender, thin-boned with boyish black hair. They said she was dating some boy over from Elmhurst but we never saw him. She lived in that house up there on the hill with her mother and an older woman who could have been her grandmother, but they didn't talk to us either. The only time I ever saw her was on the bus, probably coming back from school, or a job.

Why would Terrance think she was a gorilla? She didn't have any hair on her except for her head and her eyebrows. She didn't have long arms or a bulging forehead. Her gait was steady and her gaze was pleasant. There didn't seem to be anything dark or sinister about her. But she was always alone, getting off the bus, eating at the corner lunch counter, pushing a cart down the aisle at Key Food.

On some Saturdays I would see her with her mother on their front lawn working at their geraniums, but when they looked down the handball wall and saw me staring up at them, they wouldn't wave or even blink. The grandmother was only seen occasionally getting into a car or sitting in the third floor window, watching like a sentinel. When I was little, I would be scared of seeing her in that perch and I had to grow up to realize she was just an old lady whose life had come down to sitting in a window, more to be pitied than feared.

At night after the street lamps had turned on and everyone in the Manor was settled in their living rooms, you could see the television lights flickering in the row houses. In Maria's house, there was always a night light burning in the third floor window, and I always imagined that was where the grandmother sat without a television feeling the passage of time, accompanied by an old radio that broadcast tunes from another decade, ball games from a vanished Brooklyn, swing bands from ballrooms now abandoned, comedians feuding with scripts in hand, radio signals from Manhattan towers. Old people, I knew from the start, were comforted and kept company by their radios, whose transmissions offered something more painfully nostalgic than the television shows that cluttered the night air. Radio was the ghost that danced around the living air waves.

That summer, Terrance's family asked me to baby sit for him. He was only five and had so much energy that he often ran off and disappeared into the cellar pits of the backyard. It would take me a long time to find him. I often had to shout silly things like, "I see Terrance's belly button!" and listen for his giggle. Then I had to fish him out of the cellar pit. I finally rigged up a system where I would tie a rope to one of his belt loops and the other end to the old elm tree behind the Columbari apartment. He would run around, playing with his imaginary companions, chasing them, and the rope would swivel around the tree giving him a wide circumference in which to move. That day he had on his Apollo 11 t-shirt and I told him that we were going to land on the moon. He stepped around like he had on big heavy moon boots and spoke into his hand like it was a microphone. With a few rocks and sticks he set up moon base. The tree, of course, was the rocket ship. I put him up on the first branch and he found that thrilling, but when I told him that he was blasting off into outer space he got scared so I took him down.

"Terrance," I asked. "Why did you call Maria Tratore the Gorilla Girl?"

He was having fun, so he didn't pay much attention to my question. Finally, he lifted up his imaginary space helmet and said with a smile, "She turns into a gorilla." Then he went back to preparing for lift-off, as if what he had just said was the most casual thought in the world.

Mike and Kevin found me playing with Terrance and offered to keep me company, so we parked ourselves on the grassy knoll by the elm tree like a bunch of picnickers and let the kid play in his imaginary moon base. I told them the story about how Terrance had called Maria the Gorilla Girl, and we got to talking about her.

"He must have watched some Tarzan movies on TV," Mike offered.

"You mean Jane," Kevin said. "But she was a girl, not a gorilla."

Early morning television for kids reran the Tarzan movies, and we watched more for Jane than Tarzan. She was human, but also a creature of the jungle: the daughter of an explorer who got kidnapped by savages, then rescued by Tarzan who could barely speak English, left off his verbs. They eventually raised a family, but I never saw their saga in any sequential order. The random broadcasts of the movies showed me a story that was shuffled, in which main characters changed actors, supporting players danced between roles, and photographic texture changed. One time a silent version starring Elmo Lincoln was shown on PBS, and Tarzan was then truly mute, incapable of speech. His world was one of celluloid scratches and missing frames, accompanied by a dull piano that tinkered along moodily.

All these fragments came together over time. It was as if someone had cut everything into pieces and tossed it up in the air, then I got to follow the story in the random order in which the pieces had fallen. But once I had seen all the pieces, I could mentally rearrange Tarzan's story. And always there was Jane. She was beautiful, beleagured, scared, and often brave.

I first spoke to Maria when she got a job behind the counter at Kressler's Candy Store. My friends and I would stop by for cheeseburgers, and sit up on the stools, spin about for fun, feel under the counter for the hundreds of hard lumps that were discarded pieces of gum, order our food and then race for the comic book rack. The short order cook made the hamburgers while Maria engaged us in conversation, often asking us how things were going at the school. She had gone there ten years ago, and we were surprised to find that we had some of the same teachers.

I never asked her about Gorilla Girl. It never occurred to me that it had any existence outside of Terrance's imagination. Maria didn't look or act like a gorilla and I figured it would be a wicked insult to ask her about it. But I did get to be somewhat friendly with her. I was a few years older than the other kids who came round, and the older ones went to the shop up on Northern Boulevard that had more magazines and where it was easier to buy cigarettes.

Maria started seeing some boy her age, and I would see the two of them at the movie theater on Saturday afternoons. In a sense, I saw *Jaws*, *Superman*, *Airport '75*, *Earthquake* and *The Towering Inferno* with Maria, although we didn't sit next to each other. Her boyfriend was named Eric, and he was small and insecure, but they seemed suited to each other. There was nothing flashy or sexy about them. No surprise that they would eventually marry and spend the rest of their lives together, unsoiled by scandal, always faithful to each other, attached to sensible and sustainable jobs, living in the Manor having bought into the insider price when the whole development went condo in the '80s. They live there still, with their two children, sitting on the front porch of their unit within half a block of the handball wall and the house on the hill that has been dark and silent for many years, the mother having moved on, the grandmother having died, no other relatives having come forward to stake any claim; the neighborhood had yielded to a new generation that could not remember the 1940s or hear the strange symphonies on the antique radio, now sadly silent.

THE CANDY STORE—
COOL ENOUGH

Vinny Paganini stood outside the candy store on 20th Avenue. He was six feet tall. He had been six feet tall since he had left junior high school, but now he was out of school and he was a man all his own, with his own apartment, the one-bedroom that his mother had left him in her will, and a car all his own, a blue 1978 Ford Malibu with fin tails, which was parked outside his apartment on 19th Road. He could stand outside the candy store that his father used to take him to when he was growing up. He had always known it as Pop's candy store, but now he was his own man, and it was now his candy store, and he was there to buy cigarettes and get a hamburger at the lunch grill. He stood outside under the metal shield with the Coca-Cola logo and smoked a cigarette and tapped his sneakers against the pavement. When he was a kid, he always knew he would one day get old enough and cool enough to hang outside this candy store and be his own man.

The Saturday afternoon was progressing, and the families moved in and out of the Key Food, squeaking their small home shopping carts that they pushed for blocks. Vinny's earliest memory was helping his mother fold up that little shopping cart and hook it onto the front of the big shopping cart they had at the supermarket. The Key Food dominated the row of stores that also included the barber shop, the pizza place, the dry cleaners and the

Manor Lounge, the small bar where dirty smelly old men drank their whiskey and smoked their cigars before stumbling home at dusk. That end of the block where the Lounge resided was dark and ugly, filled with heavy air and sad men. This end of the block, anchored by the candy shop, was bright and cheerful and full of children chewing on their Milky Way and Three Musketeer bars and drinking their cans of Shasta.

Vinny tossed his butt and entered the store, pulling the door outwards and entering like a homecoming conqueror. Inside, Dave worked the lunch grill making his hamburgers and he lifted his face for a brief moment of recognition. Ever since Vinny could remember, Dave was behind that grill, and he would sit on the raised stools spinning with his legs in the open air, sliding his hand under the counter to feel the hard crusts of frozen gum, wads that had been stuck under there for decades.

Vinny didn't expect Dave to say anything, since Paganini was just another kid who used to eat his french fries but was now grown-up and looked too tall and gangly. Dave's face was lined and his hair was gray and according to his own testimony he had hair growing in places he didn't think possible and dull aches appearing in joints he didn't even know he had. But he had a small place by the airport and he cooked greasy burgers at Pop's candy store and probably did something illegal on the side with Big Ben. You could never tell with these guys, but Vinny loved him anyway and occasionally came into the store for a Dave Special, the burger, the deep fried fries and the small conic section of sweet Coke in a metal holder that made the drink look like an hour-glass.

Over to the side, across from the lunch counter, were the magazine rack and the candy rack. Both were infused with a pungent nostalgia. Vinny didn't know why the pangs came on so bad, because the racks were still there, the comic books, news magazines and candy bars were still there, but they were different. The covers of the Marvel comics were changed, and the numbers of the issues were too high. When Vinny first entered Pop's candy store and bought his first Spider-Man and Fantastic Four comics, they were 12 cents and had pop-art covers. All the issue numbers were under 100. Now they looked different, drawn more carelessly, and they were 75 cents apiece, an outrageous and unpardonable sin against kids. Vinny still had all those old super-hero mags under his bed in a cardboard box, although he hadn't read them in years, but once they were all the world to him. Those stories made him want to be a hero and fight in Vietnam, but he never got so lucky. He tried to hide his love for those mags from his friends since that meant he was a geek. They were his guilty pleasure. These new comics weren't for him, but for the little kids who came in and stared at them and waited for the right moment to steal them from under the nose of the cash register girl.

Up at the top of the magazine rack, far from the grasping fingers of small kids, were the dirty magazines with brown wrappers across their covers, like he had never seen breasts before. He didn't have any interest in them since they were filthy. Heroes didn't become heroes by getting addicted to crap like that. You had to keep your energy to yourself, not shoot it all over your sheets. Vinny Paganini was going to marry the woman he loved and take her on a trip to Sicily, and there he would lose his virginity. It would be worth the wait. He imagined it all the time and told it to all the girls he dated. He would take Mrs. Paganini to Sicily and stay with Uncle Vittorio at the Villa he remembered from a childhood visit. It was a dark room, and there was a cousin with water on the brain. He was afraid to go in there, but it was sunny outside and there were olive trees everywhere. He had never seen it so green.

A man came in through the front door, tinkling the bell. Vinny looked up and felt something fall out from beneath him. Something was wrong. Sheldon, Shelley. A weird wave passed and he looked into the face, that curved-up lip, that slightly crooked nose, the tiny birthmark on the left side of the chin. And the way he walked, upright and with purpose. It had to be a dream, a hallucination. Sheldon Blake couldn't be coming into Pop's, not like this. He was grown up and taller but it was the same Sheldon who Vinny went to junior high school with, the one who went off to the city to go to tenth grade. They moved, the whole family moved to…where?

Sheldon was standing just past the door, scanning the place

like it was a freaking dream. He walked to the comic book racks and ran his finger over the wood grain, then turned to the rotating stand of cheap toys like he was in Macy's at Christmas. There wasn't exactly joy and childish glee on his face, more like a confused and prolonged effort to concentrate and to remember something that was just out of the range of the human mind but that the comic books and toys were helping to bring into focus. Vinny knew this because he felt this way every time he came into Dave's, only it must have been more profound for Sheldon because Sheldon hasn't been here in ten freaking years.

He had on a cloth cap and a light brown jacket and couldn't get his eyes off the plastic whistles and police hand cuffs. He then tore his eyes away to look at the counter and the cash register, then walked slowly to the counter and took off his cap. He nodded to Dave who didn't recognize him, then sat down on the stool. A moment later Dave asked him what he wanted and Sheldon said something very strange.

"What do I want?" he asked, then answered. "I want to see my grandmother walking her old dog on a lost 1971 afternoon. I want to see the tide of time follow the moon back out into the bay."

"Well, we don't have that," Dave said, and turned away like he had much better things to think about.

Sheldon, I'll be damned. Sheldon.

The Pilots in Their Planes

Part One

The Brother and Sister knew it was time to land. Like pilots strapped into a cockpit and going on automatic, they felt no control over their destiny. They rode purple flames through the strangely familiar atmosphere, hurtling toward continents and oceans.

As they sank into deep sleep, their minds became deserts, the sand turning a yellow hue, reducing large purple boulders to smashed powder, dissolving into the landscape like sugar cubes in clear water. Then a mighty storm whipped up the newly formed desert floor, filling the air for miles with yellow grains, small particles of purple Sulphur chips, and long streamers of hot jell.

Through the angry tempest came an inhuman moaning sound, pervading the atmosphere, a cry of pain from some ethereal source, as if the very desert itself was groaning in sorrow. Dark forms rose and fell in the whirlwind, speechless demons flickered into manifestation, using the stormy sands as raw material for their images.

The howl of the wind becomes a large airplane roaring overhead on its way back home. The desert fades to an empty street, the sand becomes concrete, the boulder reformed as apartment houses, the purple sun settles and gives rise to a new star, a twinkling point in the moonlight...

Next came the shapes that were strangely familiar: the curve of a street corner, the silhouette of a lamppost, the trailing of telephone lines through the sky, empty doorframes and spectral doorknobs hovering in space, red bricked cornerstones, cracked sidewalk tiles, squares of concrete against a garage door, a plot of grass and a single gnarled tree riddled with bent nails...a long forgotten dream buried in the memory called Sorrow.

Demons become streets, angels scatter and leave behind clapboard houses on empty streets, the moans of sorrow wail over baseball diamonds and large fields of weeds and broken glass... rows and rows of public buses resting in hangers...the cracked airport runway by a large silent highway...

A long forgotten dream buried in the memory called Sorrow.

The Brother and Sister gasp in horror, their minds seized by an unspeakable Beauty.

They remember.

Part Two

January 14, 1988. The bus moves like a ghost through the mist-shrouded streets. Shadows move in the playgrounds over rubber mats and handball courts. Overhead the roar of jets cracks the sky. A bus depot, a candy store, the stone wall near the compost heaps.

James meets me at the bus stop, older, but the face is still the same. I haven't walked on these concrete squares in twelve years, and last time James was on his bike that still had training wheels, not even out of the third grade. In my pocket I have a photograph of him I snapped in 1974, just a small boy not yet ten playing with toys on a floor in a long vanished living room.

The row houses against the Bay...the garbage dumpsters...the supermarket and laundry, all the same. The sky is still dark. I have memories of a black sun over the concrete airport runways.

We stand at the edge of the Bay, where the sewer empties out. Across the expanse of water is the prison island, still sitting mysterious and evasive. This is the spot where I stood and strained my eyes for a glimpse of what was on the other side of the runways.

James points to the sky: "Here comes another 747 in for a landing." Already we could hear the hiss and whistling of the engine. "What marvelous machines," he muses. He wants to be an astrophysicist and build miraculous time machines.

"Where would you go in a time machine?" I asked.

"Into the past, a little into the future. Not too far though," he laughs. "I'd go a few weeks at a time, so I won't be vaporized in any atomic war."

"I'd just go back a little bit," I confessed. "I'd come right back here, to this very spot, and watch my grandmother walk her old dog that died in 1971."

We move along the lip of the Bay, tracing the deposits of sludge and oil washing up on the rocks. I point toward the sewer tunnel and say with a chill down my spine, "I once had a bad experience there."

The roar of an airplane gets louder and we stare up at the dark cloud banks swirling in unnatural formation. Far below, under the shelf of the sky, teenaged baseball players run around the diamonds of the ballfield. They look up too as the noise becomes unbearable.

"What the heck is that?" James shrieks.

There is a loud cracking noise that splits the cloud banks and a purple object hurls from above, spewing orange and crimson flames behind it like a trail of fiery lava.

"Get down!" I push James to the ground and throw my body over him, but the impact of the projectile hurls both of us up in the air, over the rocks, and into the four foot deep infected waters of the Bay.

Before long, fire engines, police cars, ambulances and most of the population of the Bay area are at the scene, keeping plenty of distance between them and the large smoking crater in the middle of the ballpark.

James wipes mud and industrial sludge from his face. "I can't believe it! I haven't seen anything like that!"

We never get near the wreck. Representatives of NASA and the US Government seal off the area and relocate the neighboring residents to detention camps. James and I live for a week in a burlap tent overlooking a highway and shopping mall and only hear the whispered rumors that spread like wildfire through the compound.

Many say it was a spaceship that crashed and that the only

surviving member was a small boy, about ten years old. He was perfectly healthy and well proportioned, but his skin was a deep orange. Others say there was a girl on board, but she had been torn to shreds by the crash.

James sat bleary eyed on a packing crate, a general issue blanket covering his shoulders and a plastic cup of hot cocoa in his hands.

"They can't fool me," he said proudly. "It was a time machine!"

Letter on Stuyvesant High School to the New York Press

I was fascinated by Ned Vizzini's article on Stuyvesant High School in the January 22 issue. I attended Stuy High myself from September 1978 to June 1981 but remember a school very different from the one Mr. Vizzini describes in his article. His Stuyvesant is a colossal edifice wedged between a river and a highway, in the shadow of the Wall Street skyscrapers, where mercenary students pursue their academic honors with the rigor and endurance of grunts at a marine corps training school. They lust for the grades, they placate their tense frustrations with drugs and skateboards, they dye their hair and surrender to the disaffected behavior of the Generation-X stereotype.

This is not the Stuyvesant that I remember. My memories have their share of pressure and grades, purple-haired nihilists, skateboarders, potheads, nerds and drug dealers. But something in Mr. Vizzini's description is either missing (perhaps he just chose to ignore it), or (and this would sadden me terribly) it just doesn't exist there anymore. That is the Stuyvesant student, of which I was one, who approached life, school and grades with a great sense of joy and creativity. We were, after all, in Greenwich Village. The Village was our campus. During cut classes, lunch breaks, or after 3:00 p.m. we took off into the streets, roaming down to

Astor Place and St. Marks to visit bookshops, record stores and Indian restaurants on 6th St. We passed under the Washington Square arch to the West Village where off-Broadway theaters and repertory houses showed double bills of foreign films. We wandered into Chinatown for authentic Asian food. We had our favorite head shops, performance spaces, dance clubs. I saw Robert Fripp perform at the Kitchen, New Order at the Ukranian National Home (even before their first album was released), Ravi Shankar at St. Mark's Church.

Even within the school, we had our alternative education. A funky physics teacher turned my group of friends onto the Tibetan Buddhist teachings of Trungpa Rinpoche. He walked me into an anarchist bookshop and ordered me to read *Nova Express* and *Naked Lunch* by William Burroughs. We ran the track in gym class while discussing surrealist art. A class trip was scheduled to see the new Kurasawa movie at the 8th St. Playhouse. We sat on the front steps reading Allen Ginsberg, Jack Kerouac, Gary Snyder. A drug dealer I knew (he sold only acid and only to friends) wouldn't sell so much as a sugar cube until his customers read *The Door of Perception* by Aldous Huxley and *Cosmic Trigger* by Robert Anton Wilson and then subjected them to an interview to see if they were mature enough to experience an acid trip. A film class in the English department showed students works by Eisenstein, Luis Buñuel and Jean-Luc Goddard. A math teacher talked to us in the hallways about quantum physics and its relationship to ancient Chinese philosophy. Many kids outside the school sat around reading *The Tao of Physics* and *Gödel, Escher, Bach*. The walls outside the school were graffittied with yin yang symbols and anarchist A's.

And the music. Within one year of attending the school, I had discovered John Cage, Brian Eno, Robert Fripp, Syd Barrett, the Residents, the Velvet Underground, Gong, King Crimson and early Talking Heads. The neighborhood was pregnant with small record shops, most of them long since obliterated. Our t-shirts didn't have sayings like "My name is Satan" or "God Is Gay" but rather "All is One" and "God is Eno."

The school had a major impact on my life. It turned me into a writer and gave me a life-long passion for cinema and experimental music. What explains the absence of any hint of this creative stimulation in Mr. Vizzini's article? Did the high school's move from the Village to Wall Street drain the sense of creativity from its students and teachers, or does Mr. Vizzini, who may not know what it's like to cut class to go see a play by Antonin Artaud on 3rd street, fail to see such an energy still alive in the school today? Did the Reagan/Bush years change things so dramatically that all traces of gnosis and art have been killed in Stuy High forever?

I haven't set foot in either building in 15 years, so I'm not the one to say. I just have Mr. Vizzini's article to clue me in. I hope he graduated with good grades and gets a decent job so he can afford an apartment in Manhattan. Since the school, in its Greenwich Village incarnation, turned me into a writer, I can't afford it.

Richard Behrens
Summer 1997

Musings on A Hard Day's Night

I recently had the opportunity to view the Beatles' film *A Hard Day's Night*. It was the first time I have seen it in its entirety since I was a teenager, and the first time I saw it on the big screen of a theater, and not on television cut with commercial breaks. Looking at it from my middle-aged point of view, the first thing I observed was that essentially the Beatles are portrayed as children. When confronted by an upper class snob in a railroad car, they taunt him with the phrase, "Mister, can we have our ball back?!" During the Can't Buy Me Love romp on the big lawn, they say to the man who owns the property, "We're sorry we hurt your field, Mister!" – both phrases that we associate with unruly kids who wander onto your front lawn to play. Instead of drinking beer, urinating on the grass, or jumping on the hoods of cars, they are merely dancing around and play-fighting each other like elementary school kids during recess. Both times we're supposed to find it charming that their anti-establishment antics do not involve destruction of property or the burning of national flags, or unlicensed sexual perversion, but merely result in a bunch of undisciplined man-children running around in a way that entertains us, especially when the film is sped up to make them look like silent film comedians. For all their parading and attempts to defy authority, they don't do anything that challenges the film's G rating. They are essentially just playfully disobedient.

The reaction of many of the authority figures to the Beatles is very much in line with this image of them as children. The television director is snobby and full of himself ("I have an award. It's on the wall in my office!"), but we can't blame him for being upset that the Beatles have vanished from the studio 20 minutes before rehearsal. We can't blame their manager, Norm, for getting angry when they don't answer their fan mail, or they disappear every time he turns his back. Norm is aptly named, since he is the normal behavior that the Beatles are deviating from, and the issue of Norm's height, with Norm being continually bothered that his assistant is taller than him ("Stop being taller than me!"), shows his inferiority complex as a parent. John Lennon's continual antics slowly contribute to Norm's nervous breakdown ("I've considered a ball and chain, but he'll just rattle them in my face, mocking me!"), and the various establishment figures that populate the film (magazine reporters, advertising executives, film studio technicians) cannot keep up with the snappy comebacks and down-to-earth dismissal of their values that the Beatles represent. When George Harrison is brought into the offices of teen idol Susan Gentry, he is repulsed by the thought of endorsing shirts that he wouldn't be caught dead wearing. It doesn't matter if the shirts are well tailored or actually nice; the idea is that the Beatles' sense of style, whether it be their German underground haircuts, or their "mocker" gear (two years earlier the Beatles had been playing in leather jackets and cowboy boots; now they are enclosed in suits and ties but with none of the trappings of Pete Townsend's sarcastic nationalism), conveys the Beatles are their own people, existing in a world apart from the trends and fads that are so carefully controlled by the media ("Can he be an early warning?" the ad exec says about George, then consults a calendar and says, "The change won't come for three more weeks!").

In reality the Beatles are being manipulated by the media, and their fashions and haircuts being marketed and sold. By the time the Fab Four had hit the silver screen, they were Pre-Fab as in Pre-Fabricated. The film *A Hard Day's Night* had removed the violent teeth once exposed by John Lennon in a Munich night club when he urinated on stage with a toilet bowl around his neck and danced drunk with prostitutes. The boys of *A Hard Day's Night* are not so much defying authority, as they are hassling a few authority figures in their daily life, not the larger authority that is reaping huge rewards from their music and milking their image in the press. In spite of all the childish and playful images they project in the film, someone in high authority is paying for the hotel rooms and the television equipment in the studio. The Beatles are only allowed near the means of production because a higher authority allows it, not because they have an innate right to be there, and certainly not on their own terms.

There is also an ambiguity over their sexuality. They leer and flirt with the dancing girls in the studio, give strange hints that they are getting aroused, but when hordes of screaming girls run after them, ready to nearly gang rape them, they run like hell, dashing in and out of limos and phone booths. They seem completely uninterested in their own fans. These girls exist to scream and yell and run after them. What divides the dancing girls in the studio from the girls in the street who are possessed by Beatlemania? The studio girls seem to be older, more womanly, while the girls in the street are plain and wear glasses and frumpy coats. One would think that if the Beatles are the randy goat-gods that mythologists portray them as, instead of running from the large crowd of girls, they would stop, turn around, and try to get their phone numbers. Perhaps they are dissuaded by what happened to Dionysus, whose fanatical female followers, in ecstatic frenzy, would tear to bits anyone who rejected him.

The film leaves questions for the viewer to solve, or at least ones that remain mysteries to me. When Ringo is alone, wandering the streets, where are the Beatlemaniac girls? And why is Paul's grandfather clean?

DAVID BOWIE LIVE:
BEFORE AND AFTER ENO

David Bowie is a performer who has always drawn upon magic and mysticism to enact his art. His pantheon of theatrical alter egos (Major Tom, Ziggy Stardust, Aladdin Sane, the Thin White Duke), his shamanic use of stage craft to propel audiences into an altered reality, his surreal science fiction lyrics and suggestive occult references, elevated him above the average glitter rock star of the '70s. Bowie was the extra-terrestrial who fell to Earth, the Gnostic alien who had been to higher planes through the use of drugs, magical practices and strange sex, ready to bring visions and wisdom to the human race through the vehicle of rock and roll.

His concerts were acts of ceremonial magic, his transmogrified body painted with sci-fi make-up ("screwed up eyes and screwed down hairdo"), morphing through different personas and states of consciousness. As Rogan Taylor commented in his excellent study of show business and shamanism, *The Death and Resurrection Show: From Shaman to Superstar* (1985), Bowie was the "man-woman about to take to the air," his Ziggy Stardust shows were "a purely magical drama revolving around the three worlds...[it's] central dramatic device: the transformation of the hero into a fantastic hero-form," and his *Diamond Dogs* concept was the "archaic shamanistic marriage of man and beast." By the time Bowie had become a rock star, he had studied Tibetan Buddhism and presumably had more than passing acquaintance with Magick (he tipped his hat to both Aleister Crowley and the Golden Dawn in his early song "Quicksand"). When he chanted the word "Ch-ch-ch-changes!" in one of his pop songs, he was not kidding around.

For a while, in the loopy swirl of the early '70s, he embodied the merging of pop culture and shamanic mysticism in an industry that was already awash with pop mysticism. Concept albums like *Ziggy Stardust* and *Diamond Dogs* unfolded like the soundtracks of fantastical movies that had never been filmed. References to Kubrick's *2001: A Space Odyssey*, *Clockwork Orange* and the novel *1984*, his well-known use of William Burroughs' cut-up technique to generate lyrics, and his name dropping of Kahlil Gibran, Andy Warhol, and Bob Dylan gave the *Cracked Actor* an apostolic authority from a much larger paradigmatic cultural context.

His ambiguous sexuality enabled both male and female fans to vent their lust in a non-threatening way; his simulated fellatio on stage with guitarist Mick Ronson, his body fitting tights and envelope pushing nudity, and his provocative revelations to the press about his "tri-sexuality" further mystified his eroticism and put him several layers of transgression beyond anything rock had seen before. Throughout much of the 1970s he was rock and roll's cosmic shaman, highly theatrical, full of mystery, and endlessly original.

However, something had happened to David Bowie by the later part of the decade. He had wiped the lightning bolt off his face, moved to West Berlin and was producing obscure post-modern electronica, hobnobbing with the likes of Brian Eno and Robert Fripp, two musical intellectuals who combined the alchemy of the recording studio with chic European experimentalism and obscure mysticisms (Eno professed an interest in the Mystical Kabala and Fripp quit music altogether in the mid-'70s to join a Gurdjieff group). Like Thomas Jerome Newton, the character he played in *The Man Who Fell to Earth*, Bowie was disappearing behind a shifting façade of designer clothing and creative decadence.

The albums *Low*, *Heroes*, and *Lodger*, known to Bowie fans as the Berlin Trilogy, were colder, more distant and minimal, less easy to interpret than his earlier work. The differences between the Bowie of 1972 and the Bowie of 1979 were profound, like the difference between Marcel Marceau and Marcel Duchamps, one full of amusement and magic who leaves children dazzled wonder-filled, the other alienating and mercurial, swathed in personal vocabularies and arcane techniques. What had happened to Bowie? Was this elegantly dressed dude of postmodern music and electronic ambiance just another one of his theatrical masks?

To make things even more confusing, Bowie ended the decade duetting with Bing Crosby on a television Christmas special, comically bantering with the aging crooner and revealing that he was just as comfortable lounging in a family living room with a log thrown on the fire, singing carols and enjoying some eggnog, as he was trancing out in a Berlin nightclub, distorting his consciousness with sex and strange drugs. Bing Crosby, oddly enough, was greatly impressed with Bowie, calling him a fine clean-cut lad and trading home phone numbers with him (Der Bingle died one month later so this collaboration was never pursued). What was it about Bowie that enabled him to trade masks so easily, even if it was the illusionary mask of having no mask? In 1980 when he recorded one of his strongest albums, *Scary Monsters*, he presented his "true face" behind all the masks: a Pierrot clown pulling off his mask to reveal more make-up and more clown faces.

Who was David Bowie? What was his true face? By comparing the Bowie of the early '70s to the bleached blond super star, ten years later, who strutted in Armani suits for his *Serious Moonlight* tour, one can see that the actor playing the character of David Bowie had undergone some unique transformation, perhaps changing with the times, perhaps following marketing strategies to sell records. Either way, he was not one to stay the same from one year to the next. Part of the endlessly fascinating appeal of David Bowie was his ability to magically morph and to hide his true personality and selfhood at the center of some elaborate maze that was never meant to be solved.

Which brings us to the CD releases of two of Bowie's live albums from the '70s, *David Live* (1974) and *Stage* (1978). Although originally released on vinyl a scant four years apart from each other, they stand at opposite ends of that transformation that shocked and alienated his original fan base.

David Live is nicely repackaged in a fold-out CD cover accommodating two disks and a booklet full of lush photographs from the concert at Philadelphia's Tower Theater. It also includes an illuminating essay by career-spanning Bowie collaborator Tony

Visconti who produced the album and who comes clean about the re-recordings that were necessary to preserve the integrity of the music. Featuring an extraordinary line-up of musicians including Michael Kamen, Luther Van Dross, David Sanborn, and Earl Slick (all of whom went on to impressive solo careers of their own), Bowie is caught in the spotlight without his Ziggy or Aladdin masks, abandoned by the Spiders From Mars, prancing about in a polka dotted shirt with red suspenders and red hair like a Southern California mall mime, portraying the character known simply as David, your host for the evening's delights, visibly the same clown who once upon a time sang amusing songs on the BBC about "Laughing Gnomes" and stoned space men.

But despite the show biz surface, the extraordinary surrealism of these songs would be a hard sell to Bing Crosby. With the exception of a few R&B soul tunes (like Ray Cropper's "Knock on Wood") that look forward to Bowie's *Young Americans* album, the set list is top heavy with material from *Diamond Dogs* and *Aladdin Sane*, a phantasmagoria of dreamscapes and fragmented imagery. Perhaps some of the songs like "Panic in Detroit" and "Suffragette City" are so familiar to us now that we have long ceased meditating upon the lyrics, but when you hear them fresh after such a long decade away from them, they really come across strange and wonderful. And dark as hell.

Unlike the early Bob Dylan who had stripped his act of all theatrical pretense and stood before audiences as a self-righteous social commentator, Bowie had a very different message: "The times they are a'telling, and the changing isn't free....Beware the savage jaw of 1984." He is dark, violent and full of black imagery, from the apocalyptic cityscapes of "Diamond Dogs," through the drug addiction and vampirism of "Sweet Thing/Candidate" to the pessimistic solitude of "Rock N' Roll Suicide," Bowie was no light weight song writer, and perhaps *David Live* loses a bit since we are denied the full visual experience of the stage show, but the songs, presented out of the context of their concept albums, as if David is trying to market his hits to a Las Vegas audience, shine like dark gems. Listen carefully. Crack open the old vinyl gatefolds and recover the lyrics in printed form. Follow along and see how full of tension and horror these songs really are, as if the painted mime has seduced us into his tent of balloons and funny animals, and then slammed the door shut behind us as he unleashes his hell hounds and black visions of a despairing future.

These may not be the best performances of the included songs, they may be rock stadium slick, overdubbed to perfection, lacking in the rawness we witnessed in the Ziggy Stardust documentary, but it is refreshing and revelatory to hear them again, thirty years later, through a musical telescope as 1974 accelerates behind us like a shooting star.

David Live represents the last manifestation of the old Bowie, the sci-fi alien with the multiple personalities and Gnostic visions. Shortly after, he would record *Young Americans* and *Station to Station*, two albums that bridge the gap of his inner transformation as an artist. It was *Station to Station* that caught the ear of the man I like to call "The Ghost in the Machine," the haunted shadow lurking behind so many of the major innovations in rock music during the '70s and '80s, that alchemical wizard of the recording studio, Brian Eno, the man who is everywhere and nowhere (he rarely broadcasts his own presence outside of liner notes and songwriting credits). In turn, his album, *Another Green World*, had mesmerized Bowie, and perhaps it was Bowie's careful listening to Eno's music that turned his mind and creative aspirations back toward Europe.

I define Eno as alchemical because during this period he was literally transforming the creative energies of musicians as he produced them. As bands like the Talking Heads, U2, Devo and countless others would reach the boundaries of their creative potential, Eno would suddenly appear in their lives like some holy guardian angel come to guide them on the sun path. He would enter into the life of the band, maintain a large degree of creative input, in many cases co-writing songs and playing instruments, infusing their work with the magical energy required to record their most profound, most inspired and most enduring albums. For example, the song "One" from U2's *Achtung Baby!* album (produced by Eno and recorded, coincidentally at Hansa-by-the-Wall, the same recording studio used by Bowie and Eno for much of the Berlin Trilogy) was originally composed as an instrumental titled from Eno's name spelled backwards.

The albums would be infused with a feeling of Eno, a process Peter Gabriel once labeled "Enossification." The Talking Heads

(*Fear of Music* and *Remain In Light*), U2 (*The Joshua Tree* and *The Unforgettable Fire*) and Bowie (*Low, Heroes,* and *Lodger*) would all go on to create much more famous and commercial albums, and would enjoy much higher levels of pop success in the charts, but never again would their albums be Enossified. Like any good holy guardian angel, Eno would lead them to the outer limits of the abyss, and then abandon them.

The story of how Bowie become Enossified is explicitly laid out in a small book by Hugo Wilcken called *Low* (2005) that is part of Continuum's 33 1/3rd series, each volume of which is devoted to a single classic rock album. It is significant that the editors of the series chose *Low* as a signature Bowie album. It is his weirdest, most experimental, and most puzzling album, certainly his least commercial (when the studio suits heard the master tapes, they threatened to suppress its release) but the story of how the album was recorded and what was transpiring in Bowie's personal life, is extremely revealing and lays bare the course of events.

Wilcken picks up the story with the release of *Station to Station* and shows how Bowie pre-echoed his Berlin persona with a stage show heavily influenced by surrealist cinema and an "austere, expressionistic flavour redolent of the European modernism of the 1920s," and his increasing interest in the Nazis (Bowie claimed that he was writing a screenplay about Josef Goebbels and made some misunderstood public statements about Fascism (he wanted to start his own country – a conceit that has ironic overtones to his recent attempts to build an elaborate on-line web community and to start his own bank)). Most importantly, Wilcken describes the effect that occult beliefs and practices were having on Bowie's state of mind and his art.

David Bowie's relationship to the occult has always been explicit. In "Quicksand" (1971), he states boldly, "I'm closer to the Golden Dawn/Immersed in Crowley's uniform of imagery." And in "Station to Station" (1976) he lets the cat out of the bag with the line, "One magical movement from Kether to Malkuth" and indeed published a picture of himself reclined on the floor drawing a Tree of Life with colored chalk. Bowie himself claimed that the title *Station to Station* was a reference to the stations of the cross, but it is more reasonable to assume that the singer is driving "like a demon" from Kether to Malkuth.

Although these are his most famous and most oft-quoted occult references, magical sensibilities permeate almost everything he did in the early '70s. The emphasis on being a rock and roll star with the emphasis on "star" ("Every man and every woman is a star" is a fundamental tenant of Crowley's mytho-poetic philosophy), and the rock star as divine being, an extra-terrestrial who has fallen from above, punctuates the spiritual aspect of his stage craft and personas. Besides, Ziggy's last name is "Stardust" and Aladdin Sane's name is not just a clever pun about mental illness, but a reference to Sufi parables and fairy tales. Also, the Thin White Duke of "Station to Station" who is throwing "sure white stains" could very well be Crowley himself who once published a scandalous book entitled *White Stains*. If one digs deeper, one can draw even tighter connections, but if you pull back to look at the wider picture, it is clear that David Bowie is a magician/shaman performing his magic both in the studio and on stage.

When Wilcken tackles Bowie's state of mind at the time of the recording of *Station to Station* and *Low*, he dips into the occult waters to describe some of the references and explain a thing or two about Sephiroths. His scholarship is not entirely stellar, since at one point he explains that Aleister Crowley shared his membership in the Golden Dawn with Henreich Himmler, who had been born in 1900 and would have been a toddler at the time that the Golden Dawn splintered into fragments. No doubt he thought there was a connection because Bowie mentioned Himmler in the song "Quicksand" right after Crowley.

Wilcken also spends some time discussing a hidden and often neglected chapter in Bowie's transformation: the recording of Iggy Pop's "The Idiot," which was produced in Berlin by Bowie and which defied explanation. Certainly much different from any work previously done by either artist, it was, as Wilcken describes, a cross between Kraftwerk and James Brown, a prototype for the gloomy debut album that was to come two years later from the Manchester cult band Joy Division, who had originally called themselves Warsaw after one of *Low*'s instrumental tracks. Bowie, who had turned toward Berlin via a meeting with Christopher Isherwood, had enlisted Iggy Pop as a sort of demented Sally Bowles to his "Herr Issyvoo."

Wilcken explains vividly how Bowie's move to Berlin was driven by his fascination with the surreal landscapes, the post-war gloom, the aura of devastation and left-over monuments from the Fascist era. The instrumentals on the second side of *Low* ("Warszawa," "Weeping Wall," "Art Decade," and "Subterraneans") all draw deeply on the dark ambiance of Berlin, the weeping despair of its dead streets and the misty decadence of its underground clubs and emerging electronic music. Further, they all share a "willingness to treat music as soundscapes, rather than structured songs with their melodic narratives."

Wilcken also describes the sources of Bowie's musical transformation. While heavily under the influence of Brian Eno's *Another Green World*, he also became transfixed by the electronic bands that he was hearing in Europe, including Kraftwerk, Neu! and Can. These bands heavily "inform" the second side of *Low* and have more than a passing influence on the short, pulsing songs on the first side, such as "Breaking Glass," "Sound and Vision," and "Be My Wife."

During the *Low* sessions, Bowie had become obsessed with what is commonly known as "magical thinking." Combining occult beliefs with cocaine is a surefire mechanism to trigger paranoia, and Bowie certainly was lacing his white powder with angels and demons. His obsessions with psychic self-defense led him to create delusions about the people he was working with. Several times recording sessions had to be stopped because Bowie was convinced a band member was performing black magic against him. Further, his marriage was deteriorating and Wilcken describes the breakdown and divorce in painful detail, putting it in the context of Bowie's worsening mental state.

But what came out of the *Low* sessions was something new, something brilliant and paradigm shifting. Poised at the cusp of the punk movement, perhaps *Low* competed on the record store shelves with an explosion of New Wave and indy label bands that were transforming the industry, but the album's long term influence is certainly apparent. Although the initial reviews were mixed (the *NME* said that the album was "stunningly beautiful if you can get past taking it as some kind of personal insult") the album grew on listeners over time. Wilcken explains, "A whole strand of post-punk owes its existence to some sort of combination of the glam-era and Berlin-era Bowie personae; to Bowie's and

Eno's injection of the synthetic into the three-minute pop song...to the album's funk/electronic hybrid; to the turn toward a European aesthetic; to the non-pop experimentalism of the second side; to *Low*'s appropriation of modernist alienation."

Indeed, Philip Glass, one of America's most esteemed composers, has fashioned *The Low Symphony*. In 2002 Bowie himself performed the album in its entirety as befitting its rank as a cultural phenomenon; and a 2-disc 30thAnniversary edition is in the works. Few fans over the age of 35 do not have each note of the Berlin Trilogy memorized in their brain stem. As time moves on, *Low*, the one Bowie album that was least likely to survive with any critical attention, has become a crucial part of rock history; and Bowie's "Berlin personae" has much to do with the album's lasting mystique.

Stage is a re-mastering of a Madison Square Garden concert that was originally released in 1978. Technically, the show was part of the *Heroes* tour and featured a good deal of live material drawn from the *Low* and *Lodger* albums. Although Brian Eno is nowhere to be found amongst the musicians, clearly he had a large hand in composing and shaping the sound of many of the songs. Hearing *Stage* directly after *David Live* is revelatory, and speaks volumes about Bowie's Enossification.

The entire first disc presents nothing but material from *Low* and *Heroes* with the exception of "Fame," which punctuates at the very end. The impact of hearing "Warszawa" live, Bowie's most artsy and noncommercial track, presented with a thundering confidence that makes the performance better in many ways than the original studio recording, is startling to an audience accustomed to the Bowie opening with a more kick-ass like "Rebel Rebel." Clearly, from the first thundering notes, this is a very different Bowie we are dealing with. The songs from *Low*, in particular "Sound and Vision" and "Breaking Glass," feel more rounded, more conceived and song-like than the original recordings. Instead of being pieced together by Bowie and Eno as a challenging studio experiment, they are here played by a polished band that has worked around the experimental forms of the songs, shaping them into something more presentable to a stadium screaming for Ziggy Stardust showstoppers.

The song "Heroes," which was originally composed and

recorded in Berlin, has references to armed guards on a wall (the recording studio Hansa-by-the-Wall where *Heroes* was recorded had windows that looked directly out onto the armed guards in the towers of the Berlin Wall) has locked that song into every Bowie fan's imagination with the disturbed politics of that war torn city. But Bowie's presentation on *Stage* is one of a polished showman, as if the personal torments, the occult paranoia, the disintegrating relationships and fractured attempts to find new musical forms, is now behind him, and he can strut his skinny stuff across a stadium stage once more, rocking out, and making the audience cream their pants.

Despite Eno's absence, other contributors help make this concert recording one of the most compelling that Bowie has ever released. The marvelous band included the Twang Bar King himself, Adrien Belew, whose wobbling guitar solos and aural pyrotechnics sound like dress rehearsals for the experimental deconstructions of melody he brought to the Taking Heads' *Remain in Light* and to Bowie's next album *Lodger*. Belew himself was only a year or two away from the exponential expansion of his talents, recording with Frank Zappa, touring with the Taking Heads, and then becoming the front man in one of the most musically awesome events of the 1980s, the reconstruction of King Crimson, where he held his own playing lead guitar with God-On-Earth Robert Fripp directing from his stage right stool. Belew is one of the great musicians of the 1980s and here, on Bowie's most powerful live album, just on the cusp of having his genius recognized, he is giving musical birth to himself.

Much of the tracks on the second disc derive from *Station to Station* and *Ziggy Stardust*. In fact, Ziggy is represented by five straight tunes in a row (I believe on the vinyl copy of *Stage* this was an entire side) which sound just as driven and exciting as they appeared in the Ziggy Stardust movie. The world doesn't really need another live version of "Hang On to Yourself" (I once joked that Bowie's next release was going to be the 4-CD *Hang On to Yourself Live* box-set), but how often are you going to hear a live version of "Soul Love" or "Five Years"?

Station to Station is represented by "TVC15," "Stay," and "Station to Station." The final instrumental ending of "Stay" is sheer electricity, transcending the original studio recording, and builds with a soaring Belewian solo to its crashing conclusion. "TVC15" is just as quirky and odd as it was when Bowie presented it on *Saturday Night Live* while dressed as an airline stewardess with a toy poodle, Klaus Nomi miming behind him.

After *Stage*, Bowie was to record his last two masterpieces, *Lodger* and *Scary Monsters* and then he put away his Japanese make-up and mime costumes for the Armani suits and the financially successful pop tunes. It was significant that after completing the *Low-Heroes-Lodger* trilogy with Brian Eno, Bowie was left with a dubious hole where his Enossification used to be. Only when he reunited with Brian Eno in 1995's *Outside* did Bowie do anything as musically innovative or self-transformative as *Low*. Fortunately, he has been a tad bit Enossified ever since.

JAIPUR

I write these notes under ceiling fans in the desert city Jaipur, lying in my thin, white, cotton Indian pants with my naked, browning toes curling around my bed's metal frame, my sun-burnt neck and reddened arms sprawled on dusty sheets. Above my head sits a wooden shelf with my shaving mirror, toothbrush, malaria pill, and a half-filled glass of warm water.

I walked the streets of this pink Maharaja city today, tell-tale tourist with my pink skin and 35 mm camera slung securely across my chest. The hot Indian desert sun beat on the back of my neck, my T-shirt quickly became a wet rag. My throat parched, I searched my pockets for change to buy water from refrigerated pump stands.

"Hello, what country you from?" The voice, loud and penetrating, coming from a large Sikh with an impressive turban, offering me a ride in his three-wheeled taxi cab. Moments later a young Indian student asks me if I wanted to sell my camera.

A welcome cool breeze blows through the pink streets, and a calm descends on me as I kneel before an emaciated pandit and touch his walking stick. He pulls at his white rags and a brief smile appears on his aging face as we share a moment of human warmth.

"Hello? You come with me?" interrupts a teenage male prostitute, his lean brown stomach exposing feminine curves, his mouth in a red lipsticked, sensuous pucker, his eyes darkly painted.

Nearby, a fat Sikh drinks from a water pump and eyes the boy lustily. In the streets, old men and women squat in groups, picking at plates of spiced food, and fingering little handicrafts that they hawk to the passing crowds.

I load film into my camera under the archway of a pink building. "Hello? You sell camera?" A brief smile appears on his aging face. There is a constant stench of human filth in the streets. I take one last photograph for human sadness: of the armless, the legless, the fingerless, all stumbling through archways in destitute cities of the world. "You stay at cheap hotel? Hello America? You come with me?"

I turn, not so willingly, into an alleyway, then through a doorway where I descend rotted wooden stairs to a concrete room where a mad woman pulls at her dirty, matted hair. I walk back 300 years, as I pass through the Mughal doorway. There is a rectangular courtyard where the Emperor plays chess with beautiful virgin girls like pieces on a huge chessboard, laid down in stone. A throng of naked boys dive into marble pools for the pleasure of the Maharaja.

Back on the street, my arms are burning raw red in the noon time sun of the desert of Rajasthan. I return to my hotel where the jug of water has become warm and putrid, unpleasant to drink. An old Rajasthani waiter carries a tray of iced water down the concrete corridor toward my room. I spend a few, long minutes trying to communicate that I would like an entire jug, not just a glassful.

But water is water here in this desert town.

Six Meals

One

   Big Grandma came to the table and the bowl was there and
there was milk in it and cereal. I opened the chocolate box and
I took the spoon and then there was chocolate on the milk and
I went to eat it and my spoon went away to the floor. I looked
down and Big Grandma came and she told me not to put more
chocolate on but she gave me a new spoon and it had Bozo on it
and I took the spoon and put it in the box and then I put the whole
thing in my mouth and the chocolate was like that. I cried and Big
Grandma came over again and she was mad. I said TV set and she
put on the cartoons and then there was Moe and then there were
living statues and they were mad at me. She told my parents that
I cried.

Two

After school, Billy, Mike, and I went over to 21st Avenue because Mike was going to be flipping cards so we stopped at the candy store and Ted was behind the grill. I ordered a Ted Burger and he made some stupid jokes. I grossed Mike out because I made him put his hand under the counter where all the dried gum was and he went, "Oh, snap!"

I got the Ted Burger with a Coke and the Coke came in the paper cone which took less time to drink but I also got the french fries that I liked with the extra salt. The burger came on a paper plate and I always took off the lettuce and tomato because they didn't taste good. The burger had a smoky taste and was good with ketchup.

The candy was up front underneath the cash register, and they had rows and rows of bars all with different colors on the wrappers. One of them had the Three Musketeers on the wrapper and another one had the words Milky Way and those two were my favorites. After a Ted Burger I liked to eat a Three Musketeers and get a can of Coke and then I would feel full.

My dad says that Ted never cleans his grill and he calls the hamburger Heart-Attack-On-A-Plate. My father is like that, he has funny things to say about everything. Like the time he called my grandmother a tub.

I bought the bubble gum cards with the Partridge Family on them and I chewed the stick of gum that came in the wrapper. There was a sugar powder on them that was like the powder that came out of the fake cigarette when you blew on it to make it look like you were smoking. Ted smoked after he made the hamburgers and we could smell it all over the store. When I'm big enough, I'm going to buy the cigarettes. There is a camel with a pyramid behind him that's really cool and the camel is smoking a cigarette.

'Then we spun around on the seats and Billy ran to where the magazines were and pretended to get the stuff on the top shelf and we all laughed. Then Mike threw his food in the air and Ted yelled and we all went running.

We stopped in the alley way behind Hale Head's house and started to flip cards and Hale Head came out. Kids didn't like him because he had warts on his fingers, so many of them that his mother called him an epidermic. He brought out some egg salad sandwiches and we started eating them but then Billy said "Eeewww!" because Hale Head had made the egg salad with his hands and that meant we were going to get his warts. He felt bad so he brought out some Hi-C and we drank it from the can and it tasted like being two years old and watching the Jerry Mahoney Show. Then Hale Head won all the cards from me and I got angry at him and jumped on his back and he spun around trying to whip me off, but I threw his glasses into the bush and so he called me an Episcopalian.

Halfway home I went to the fence where the softball field was and I started barfing. The Ted Burger and the egg salad was all over the grass. I lay on the dirt and thought of bad things like the dried gum under the lunch counter and the time that Billy's thing was hurting and he showed it to me and it looked weird.

Three

The train to Bombay was scheduled to leave Madras Station in just a few minutes and the conductor announced that there wouldn't be any meals served for the entire trip. Douglas told me to sit still and he ran off the train to get some food from the platform. We had been traveling for eight weeks and had been very careful so far about our food, especially anything shelled. We drank the government-inspected water that was sold on the street (one well-suited gentleman who watched us buy the tall glasses just laughed and said, "Government inspected!" and laughed again) and only ate in restaurants, never taking food from the farmers sitting on the sidewalks. On the trains, they served small cartons with basmati rice, a cup of dal, some chapati bread and tiny wet pieces of okra that tasted like balls of mucous. For eight weeks we had not been sick off that combination. It was a staple during the famine, someone told us, and he were grateful to have it.

Douglas came back from the platform just as the train was starting up, with two little boxes with grease stains on the sides. "Lunch," he shrugged.

As usual, our cabin was filling with farmers and entire families. They brought out their traveling kits for cooking and before long were stirring puffed steamed rice and scooping handfuls into their mouths, pushing with their fingers. They scooped with the right hand because the left hand was used for cleaning yourself after a bowel movement. I was left-handed, and often drew troubled stares from fellow passengers when I ate.

I opened my box and inspected the peppered eggs, the cup of mango slices, the plastic container of rice and dal. Something didn't look right, but we ate it. The others in the car stared at us curiously. White people never traveled second class and ate food from the platform.

The teenager in the bunk below me was a student who came from a small town in Rajasthan and he had won a scholarship to a university. He carried around a newspaper clipping that told of his lucky break. He also carried some biscuits that he shared with us. He was friendly and chatted openly, asking us where we had been, what we had seen, where we were going. He also asked us, "What is your goal?" which confused us at first but we figured out finally that he meant "What do you want to do after college?" We told him that we didn't know and he told us that he was going to be an engineer and live in New Delhi and have lots of girlfriends.

Then he looked both ways slyly before asking: "In your country, you have sex before marriage?"

"Why, yes," we said. Douglas and I were both virgins, but this conversation gave us some authority.

He giggled. "Would you draw me a picture of a naked woman?"

I took out the greasy napkin from the bottom of my lunch box, which smelled of peppers and badly cooked rice, and made a crude drawing of the female anatomy. It was sparse, barely recognizable, but it made his face grin.

That night, up in my berth, I noticed the light below me was on. The student was sitting up, holding my pornographic napkin to the light, staring at it. The clipping announcing his scholarship had fallen to the floor.

Gradually, I became aware of a tearing in my abdomen, and then it turned into a sharp burning pain as if a knife were ripping across my colon. In the bunk across from me, Douglas was groaning. We had eaten the peppered eggs from the platform, unshelled? Our outcries woke many passengers and the night conductor came running. Two men carried me to the toilet but my shorts were flooded before we got there. I lay on the filthy train floor, crying, my shaking knees drawn to my sunken chest and the conductor didn't know what to do because it was still ten hours to Bombay.

Four

I went to see Little Grandma. Big Grandma had died many years ago and Little Grandma was all I had left. She lived in an adult community north of Princeton. I had never seen so many lawn sprinklers. The building complex was immense but there were no staircases, just wheelchair ramps that dominated the hallways. The public address system piped in Benny Goodman, Gene Krupa, and Duke Ellington. As I walked I imagined my own old age home in the year 2050. 'Psycho Killer' by the Talking Heads would comfort my senility.

She lived behind the little door with the potted geranium and the brass knocker. Three minutes after I knocked she opened the door, her big Coke-bottle glasses staring up in stages, her knobby fingers adjusting the lenses and finally recognizing me.

"Yes, you. Come in before they see you."

Inside everything was the same as it had been a year ago. The furniture from the old apartment that she had shared with my grandfather was laid out in the same pattern. It was as if the old place had grown new walls. The painting of a full-rigged sailing ship over the couch still dominated the room as if at some point in the past, my grandmother had dreamed of adventure on the high sea; but it was more likely that the painting was a cheap gift from when she opened up a savings account at a bank.

We used to call her the Little General. She was full of energy and nerve; time had not diminished her. First she told me that I was looking thin and then asked me how my father was but she couldn't remember if he was her first-born son or her second. I sat with her on the couch under the British ship and listened to her talk and talk and then I tried to do some talking and then she talked again and then I tried to talk again but she offered me lunch.

"Come on, you must be hungry. I haven't seen you eat since the last time you were here."

"Yeah, Grandma, there were some meals in between there..."

"Come," she said, pulling me into the tiny little kitchenette. I looked around at the mountain of supplies. The woman went down to the cafeteria every afternoon and put things in her handbag: packets of sugar, cookies, graham crackers, a squeeze bottle of ketchup, cake. And inside her refrigerator, all that food wrapped in silver foil: chicken legs, roast beef strips, hardboiled eggs without the shells. God knows how long they'd been sitting there.

"You want some coffee," she said. "I got some instant." She poured hot water from a rusted kettle into a spotted glass and then put it down on the breakfast table. Then she took a Tupperware container that looked as if it had been closed for some time and spooned out granules of instant coffee. "Here's some milk," she said, and put a container down. There was milk inside, no doubt the booty from her pillaging of the creamers in the cafeteria, but the container was an old pickle jar and it smelled sour. I politely pushed it aside.

"You want some chicken, I just defrosted it," she said as her eyes got wider behind her Coke-bottle glasses.

With my grandmother, the word "just" was always problematic. But I had already turned down the milk, so I was doomed to eat the chicken. She microwaved the parts, all the time saying, "They say that these ovens could kill you when you stand in front of them," and then started to go on a long monologue about how she can't watch one channel on the TV set while tape recording on another.

I told her you can do that and she told me that you can't, so I dragged her into the living room area and showed her the mode button on the remote. I popped in a tape to illustrate, and the tape turned on by itself and there, before us, was my grandfather who had died three years ago. He was old, with his walker, and on his way to the bathroom. My cousin's voice behind the camera blurted out, "So Grandpa! How do you feel today?"

And my grandfather's old and sick face, sunken with the years, turned to the camera, his eyes blurred, his chin flecked with spittle, and he replied, "What does it look like?"

I turned to my grandmother and asked her if I could skip the chicken. She looked down at the television and pointed to the colored tape over the controls. "He would turn the wrong dials. You know, after his operation. He would sit so close so he could see the baseball."

Then she went to the closet and pulled down some polo shirts. "Do you want them? They look like a fit." One shirt she held out, a plaid design with epaulettes, was what he had on the day he told me that he was going to watch a W.C. Fields movie on the set. He pushed his walker into the other room saying, "I want to see what the fuss is about!" After about a half hour he came back with a sour look on his face: "I've seen funny and that's not funny." I forgot to ask him what movie he had watched. Maybe he hadn't even been on the right channel and he had been watching a news report and that's why it wasn't funny.

I went back to the living room and my grandmother pushed past me and went into the kitchenette again, ferreting through the cabinets. She asked me to reach up to the top shelf and I pulled down a Jell-O box that had an expiration date from ten years ago. "Do you want it?" she said. "You can use some food."

"No, not this."

"But you can use some food."

"Yes," I told her. "I can use some food."

Five

Here, on the bed, the calls of children shouting in Italian from the courtyard. The bedroom has no fan. I am baking in the Calabrian heat with a head full of jet lag and my wife by my side, sleeping peacefully. Then she awakens and stares at me and we look about the room, the same bedroom she remembers from her childhood, closed for years now—opened just for us. Our suitcases, travel guides, money belts and sleeping pills on a small desk under a ticking clock and old photographs from the 1920s of mustached grand-uncles who had slept in this room before the war. Their eyes follow me to the bathroom.

The small child has run up the hallway, poking her chin in through the door. I call her Mussolina because she would push out her chin and open her eyes wide. "Lunch!" she says as if having memorized the English with great care. "Mange!" Stumbling to our feet we follow her to the downstairs room where the table has been laid with plates, silverware, bottles of acqua minerale and baskets of fresh bread. The two aunts have been laboring in the kitchen for hours, preparing the pasta and meats and fish they had purchased at the city market and driven up the long mountain road to this village to prepare especially for us, the American cousins.

The uncle, noble chin, tall forehead, rolled-up sleeves on his button-down shirt with the large hands that can only come from decades of being a stone-mason, sits at the head of the table asking about English, which he can't speak. His wife carries the food to the table while the adults and children alike gather around, addressing each other in lyrical waves which I had only previously encountered in foreign films. Lacking the subtitles, I struggle to pick up key phrases, stray words, and recognizable phonemes. My wife speaks in broken Italian trying to tell them that my stomach is delicate and I shouldn't eat too much meat, but it doesn't seem like they understand her.

The first plate before me is a large slab of lasagna, steaming and dripping with fresh tomato sauce, basil and garlic. As soon as all but the women are seated, I scoop it with my utensils, resting it by my nose to sense the fresh ingredients and to prepare for my first taste of real tomato sauce. The male cousin laughs at me and presses his empty fingers to his lips to encourage me; and so I start to wolf it all down, inhaling the wavy pasta and the chunks of beef with irrational need. The hunger in my belly grows as I finish my first few bites, so I devour more, rushing the food and lusting after its textures. This is the tastiest and fullest food I've ever eaten, I admit to myself, and I had to travel to Italy to get it. I eat it completely before it's had a chance, before my stomach can admit that it's had too much, before my brain can register that a large bolus of carbohydrates and animal flesh and plant matter has been deposited into its pit. My wife places two fingers on my hand, pressing down as I attempt to scoop the rest of the sauce from the empty plate. "That's only the first course," she reminds me.

Outside the town has come awake after a sluggish afternoon in the heat. Shop fronts up and down the Via Roma have opened up, awnings elevated, doorways unlocked and reopened, tables put back on the streets. You can hear the children crying in the churchyard and mothers calling for them from balconies. The single bus to arrive from Naples each afternoon has parked in front of the house and you can hear the motor stirring. More relatives tumble in through the narrow door to the backyard, come to see the American cousins, their sun-baked faces smiling and their warm voices encouraging me to eat more, eat more.

Il Secondo. Meat. Boneless breast with bread crumbs lightly fried and stacked in a pile very high, right before me. I take one piece, eat it, and then take another. Chicken is my favorite animal meat and I have no problem eating a third piece. My wife politely takes a breast and nurses it. The uncle, the male cousin, Mussalina, the others, all take small pieces, cut it in half, take a bite then engage in conversation, subtly hinting that it is my job to clear the bottom of the plate. Before I can do that, the beef comes out, the rib steaks dripping onions into the wet plate and I take one before I have finished the third chicken breast. One of the aunts comes and yells at me, points at my plate and makes a mean face, telling me that I must eat more. I wait for her smile but she recedes to the kitchen wiping sweat from her cheeks before I am given any hint that she had levity in her commands.

The fowls of the field and the beasts of burden make way for the watery denizens, now boneless and laid open, the heads still gawking with their disturbingly familiar eyes. I cut two heads off and take the fish meat while trying to nurse the beef steak. I do take note that my wife has politely taken one slice of each animal although she is usually a vegetarian. The aunt does not poke her finger into my wife's plate, does not make the furrowed brow and wipe the sweat from her cheeks like she is impatient. My wife must be doing something right to be so little chastised. I lean to her and whisper, "I'm going to be sick," but there is nothing she can do.

The atmosphere has become more like a circus now that some neighboring dogs have come to visit without their owners, to bark and snap and try to climb up the table legs. A large man with a broad face and enormous white mustache has come to bring news but no one seems deeply affected by his grim words; then he leaves without anyone offering him a piece of meat. Two old women in their nineteenth-century head scarves and fantastically carved faces come in to sit in the corner but no one questions who they are or whether they are hungry or not. The children race about and grab morsels as they choose. The uncle sits stoic and strange with a cup of acqua before him and after, as I finish eating each discrete piece of meat, I try to buy some time by asking him if he wants more and he nods and I pour him another cupful; but as for his own food he takes barely a nibble. These odd neglects suggest the entire meal was a parade designed to gauge my endurance, to stuff hospitality so far down that I couldn't help but feel their generosity, even if it meant induced vomiting to make room for more food.

"I won't make it," I tell her, holding her hand. My wife's eyes come back with helpless empathy.

Vegetable side-dishes start to appear: marinated cauliflower, fried potatoes, sliced garden fresh tomatoes with accompanying balls of mozzarella cheese. I am now performing more a parody of eating, a fantastical waltz through the gestures and motions. The food that actually disappears into me is mere artifice, strictly theater, props in some vast game of being an American adored by Italians. I know there is more, I sense there is more. Each bite makes my wife telescope further away to a place where I cannot get at her. The uncle sits and watches, sentinel eyes that have seen the American airplanes fall over Sicily, who has cut stones from mountainsides near Monte Casino, who has never digested Rome because they never leave the mountain, like a Brooklynite who has never bothered to take the trip to the Empire State Building. In this village, the uncle can be Italy and has no need to take the bus back to Napoli and learn about the fancy ways of the opulento. "Eh!" he would say dismissively, shrugging his shoulders as he upturned his palms.

The array of meat vanishes, the vegetables and cheese disappear. An aunt appears in the kitchen doorway holding another plate. The dogs are not getting their share because the scraps are being shoveled into me. Mussalina thrusts out her chin and sings some unintelligible pop song and bangs her unused fork, then pours Coca-Cola into a plastic cup. The mechanical church bell across the yard goes off on a timer and echoes against the mountain slopes.

I grasp with greasy fingers that can hardly hold a utensil toward my wife's face, hoping to touch her, to pull her back. She sees me but cannot respond.

Six

(unfinished)

POETRY FOR ANNA

Introduction

From my first telephone conversation with Richard, I suspected that he was somebody quite extraordinary. After meeting him for the first time to watch the Beatles' film *A Hard Day's Night*, I was sure of it: I had met a modern-day Renaissance man. His was a kind and gentle spirit and he was extremely witty, even downright hilarious at times. Richard and I quickly became each other's closest friend, having thought-provoking conversations and attending cultural events together, including films, museums, historical sites, and theater, so much theater. I felt as if I knew him my whole life, like an old friend who knows you so well that much of your conversation does not have to be spoken aloud.

Richard was well versed on so many topics, but I had the unique pleasure of exposing him to nature. We spent a lot of time at our local lake with its croaking frogs and sunbathing turtles, and quietly sitting in the bird blind to witness the colorful songbirds feeding. This was novel, indeed, to a city boy like Richard, and he embraced it with the intellectual and spiritual curiosity that he brought to everything he studied. Richard even proposed to me on a hiking trail and then spontaneously carved our initials in a fence post to mark that romantic spot (so as not to harm a living tree). At that point Richard become a bona fide nature lover, and the love of my life.

The following selected poems, which are deeply personal to

me, to our love and life together, are the manifestations of our whirlwind courtship and nature experience. Richard so deftly crafted songbird and nature metaphors to represent what he was feeling in his heart and soul. I share these poems now, a year after his passing, as I want his words to give voice to those who have found their extraordinary love, as I was so fortunate to have found mine in Richard.

Anna Behrens
New Hampshire
2018

> "What though the radiance
> which was once so bright
> Be now for ever taken from my sight,
> Though nothing can bring back the hour
> Of splendour in the grass,
> of glory in the flower,
> We will grieve not, rather find
> Strength in what remains behind."

William Wordsworth

Bird Blind

(for Anna)

Our souls skirted the clouds, far from earth,
Trembling, chirping away our most secret gifts.
No seeds or nest laced our hearts.
We perched like ancient spirits in a tin cage
Watching the family crack our eggs
That stood no chance of birth.

Yet April spring brought the breaking of light
On the horizon of the turtle lake,
And with the courage of lonesome hawks
We turned our faces towards one another
And felt the plenitude of the wire
Upon which we balance.
In us, the dawn arose, and we gazed
At the sun as it cast its healing rays
Upon our thirsty faces
And with eyes
Fully open to the miracles of air

We sing together.

The Heart Shaped Home

Upon a patch of wintered earth
An elm, and a heart shaped home.
For the cardinal who frets and darts
At dawn, waiting for the sun.
She has fed here all the dark days
And bore the solitude with hope.
The seeds are scarce, the spring delayed.
With one eye she watches the woods
And waits for the leaves to part for her
To unveil the imagined return of her king.
The earth creatures make their tracks
In the remaining snow, and the finches
Watch her with suspicion, waiting for
A minute lapse in her vigilance.

Her heaven is a falling of seeds
So plentiful that it would seem that
The flowers and trees that give them
Love her with a single burning heart.
One morning, he is there, unblinking,
His red crest, his dark mask, his flaming cape.
He drops before her a single seed,
Pushes with his beak, and waits for her
To crack out its meat, and to know
That another living creature, like herself,
So alien and strange, and yet so correct,
So flawed and broken, and yet survived,
So visionary in his blindness,
Can know her, and love her, and live
With her in her heart shaped house
Forever.

The Marriage Bed

The Soul, my Love, is as real
As a golden dawn.

Upon this bed, side by side,
The very moment of falling into
Sleep promises a great and beautiful
Awakening.
A beam breaks through the muddy
Horizon, vermilion light cast
Sparks on the baked sand.
We stir, our eyes still closed,
Sensing the dawn, the first call
Of the dove in the mist.

We are two together, about to witness
The morning fire curl the lip of the distant
Shore. The stars diminish, the black of night
Surrenders to its lover, the day.

Our lids flutter, our vision greets the sun.
Look, we say, amazed and breathless.
And the marriage of night and day
Consumes our united hearts.

One Year

One glance at the cosmic ocean
We read the stars like a Book
That is teaching us a language
Spoken only by two mouths

The last time that fire chariot
Was against that twelfth of
The Zodiac, you were parading
Into my eyes and saying Yes.

The planets our stepping stones:
Mercury the spoken word,
Venus the overture and aria,
Moon our clear dream,
Mars our fiery spirit,
Jupiter our Judgment,
Saturn our wisdom.
These together will bring
The daybreak we have
Conjured with our vows.
With you I can be anyone
Because you let me be
Myself, and we scan the rest
Of our lives like a camera
recording the Sun.

About the Author

Richard was born and spent most of his boyhood in Queens. The Garden Bay Manor in Astoria was his neighborhood, where he could run freely with his friends all over the common areas of the Manor, pretending that the giant concrete planter was a spaceship, or biking down the paved paths, trying to be the first of his friends to jump the grassy hill without falling. The Riker House across the street, the bridge to the prison, Ditmars Boulevard and Steinway Street with their candy store and comics, all were fixtures in Richard's mind throughout his life. In his teen years Richard and his family moved into the Forest Hills neighborhood of Queens, and then in his early adulthood, Richard's work brought him to suburban New Jersey, although he was always a New Yorker in his heart and soul. While living in New Jersey, Richard met and married his wife Anna, and soon afterward they moved to New

England. It was in this, the happiest period of his life, that Richard was able to focus on his writing, film-making and podcasting.

Richard and Anna co-founded Nine Muses Books so they could personally publish his writings, including his *Lizzie Borden, Girl Detective* series of mysteries, for which he is best known. Richard wrote easily in many genres, in both fiction and non-fiction. His fiction short stories and non-fiction essays have been published in a variety of journals. He was also a lecturer on historic Victorian women and on silent film comedy. Richard also was a budding actor and appeared in several local plays. His *GardenBayFilms* Channel on YouTube contains a variety of short films Richard made, mostly centered on Lizzie Borden. Richard's Lizzie Borden Podcast, available on iTunes, examines the Lizzie Borden case with various historians, as well as contains a radio play of *The Agitated Eloqutionist*, one of his Girl Detective short stories.

Richard had plans to continue to create films, write stories, deliver more lecture series, and to interview more historians for his podcast, but his ill health caused him to put his plans on hold. When he learned that he did not have much time left, he said, "But I am not finished yet!" After it became tragically clear that Richard would not recover, he indicated to his wife that he wished his writing to be published posthumously. He had an idea for his most personal, and somewhat autobiographical, stories to be collected in a volume called *Garden Bay Stories*. This book is a realization of that wish, although, sadly, some of his stories were incomplete, so they appear as vignettes. The book also includes a selection of Richard's beautiful love poems written to his wife.

Anna, with the help of Richard's sister Susan, gathered Richard's writings and sorted the finished pieces into three different books: Richard's personal writings, which would be part of his *Garden Bay Stories*; his non-fiction essays, which would be part of the *Moons and Monoliths* essay collection; and his Lizzie Borden, Girl Detective stories collected into one complete volume, *The Audible Amnesiac and other Lizzie Borden, Girl Detective Mysteries*. Richard is sorely missed, but he leaves us a legacy of fine work in a variety of media and genres.